GETTING TO
SLEEP

Simple, Effective Methods for
Falling and Staying Asleep,
Getting the Rest You Need, and
Awakening Refreshed and
Renewed.

Ellen Mohr Catalano
with contributions by
Dr. Wilse Webb • Dr. James Walsh • Dr. Charles Morin

NEW HARBINGER PUBLICATIONS, INC.

Edited by Nina Sonenberg
Cover by SHELBY DESIGNS & ILLUSTRATES

ISBN 0-934986-93-2 (paperback)
ISBN 0-934986-94-0 (hardcover)

First Printing August 1990   8,000 copies

Dedicated to my parents and Grandmother Regier who taught me the positive side of stubbornness.

Table of Contents

Acknowledgments

My friends and family will tell you that sleep is one of the things I do best. While I brought to the writing of this book common sense knowledge of what makes for good sleep, I want to thank the following professional and friends who were instrumental in providing editorial support, content feedback, and encouraging words: Dr. Charles Morin of the Medical College of Virginia Sleep Disorders Center; Dr. Joseph Dane of the University of Virginia Pain Management Center; Dr. Stephen Wegener of the University of Virginia Medical School; Dr. Frank Finger of the University of Virginia Department of Psychology; Dr. Charles Holland of Roanoke, Va.; Barbara Holt, Certified Respiratory Therapist at Chippenham Memorial Hospital in Richmond, Va. And, finally, thanks to the patience and good will of my husband, Glenn, and the staff of New Harbinger Publications.

1

Introduction

Everyone has spent a miserable night or two huddled in bed endlessly rearranging the covers and wishing just to fall blissfully asleep. Temporary sleeplessness can be a normal reaction to anxiety at home or work, and for most people normal sleep returns the next night. But millions of Americans spend night after night tossing and turning, and awaken—if they sleep at all—feeling overwhelming fatigue. This may go on for months or longer. If you're one of those millions, you know the feelings of despair such sleeplessness can bring. You might worry that something is terribly wrong with your body or your mind.

It is estimated that as many as 15 to 30% of the adult population suffers from insomnia. That figure may be higher for those working odd hours or doing shift-work. Sleep difficulties rank next to back problems and colds as among the most commonly heard complaints in clinics and doctors' offices. Insomnia, Latin for "not sleep," isn't the only sleep disorder, but it is the most common.

Insomnia is a complex phenomenon, involving psychological as well as physical factors. You've probably noticed that sometimes a night without sleep can cause no ill effects. This perception usually reflects on what you have to do the next day. If you get up looking forward to the day, a sleepless night is not particularly worrisome or debilitating. But if you get up dreading some part or all of the day, a sleepless night can be the final straw. It might seem the ominous precursor to a series of bad events. Insomnia induces fatigue, of course, but it is also often associated with anxiety, irritability, and depression. These feelings may be both cause and consequence of the insomnia.

Sleep is a complicated thing, even though you do it in some form or fashion just about every night. As you will see in this workbook, there is a broad range of psychological and physical possibilities in determining what makes you sleep or not sleep well.

This workbook is intended for those suffering from both short- and long-term insomnia. Chronic or persistent insomnia is a condition that lasts two to three months or longer. Temporary or transient insomnia usually involves a sleepless night or two, typically related to situational anxiety. Sufferers of both types will find it most helpful to begin with Chapter 2, *Insomnia,* and follow it up with Chapter 3, *Sleep Hygiene.* These chapters cover the basics of the disorder, define some terms and distinctions and offer first-aid that may just solve your problem. Chapters 6 through 11 will provide you with more specific techniques for physical and emotional treatment, such as deconditioning, relaxation, and obsession management.

Insomnia is sometimes a symptom of a more serious medical problem. For this reason, Chapter 4 deals with ruling out physiological disorders, such as sleep apnea and narcolepsy. If you suspect that your sleep difficulties may be related to a chronic illness or disorder such as that chapter describes, you would be wise to consult your physician. You might also consider a specialist in sleep disorders, or make an appointment at a sleep laboratory. An up-to-date listing of sleep clinics and related organizations can be found in the appendix of this book.

In an effort to sleep "normally," you may have resorted to sleeping pills, other drugs, or alcohol, only to find that those so-called "sleep helpers" lose their effect after a while. In the long run, in fact, they *keep* you from getting restful sleep. Dr. James K. Walsh, Director of the Sleep Center at Deaconness Hospital in St. Louis, Mo., has written Chapter 5, *Medications for Sleep*. You'll find it helpful in understanding drugs and their effect on sleep.

Those of you who work odd hours, night shifts, or travel extensively in different time zones will find Chapter 11, *Circadian Rhythms and Sleep*, particularly helpful. If disturbing dreams shatter your nocturnal peace, Chapter 12 discusses dreams, specifically nightmares, and their relation to sleep patterns. Dr. Wilse Webb of the University of Florida in Gainesville has written Chapter 13, *Aging and Sleep*, for those curious about the specific changes in sleep patterns people undergo as they age. Dr. Charles M. Morin of the Medical College of Virginia in Richmond, with Dr. Sandy E. Gramling, concludes the list of contributors with a chapter written specifically for chronic pain patients and their particular sleep difficulties.

Sleep is something you once took for granted, like breathing. In childhood it was as natural as being hungry. Why does sleep change as you age? What can you do in adulthood to find restful sleep, to reprogram yourself to shed daytime worries so you can recreate the sleep experienced as a child?

Part of the answer lies in awareness and understanding of your unique sleep habits. As with undertaking any behavioral change, the first step is for you to set aside previously held beliefs and rituals about sleep. Then you will need to take action. If you follow the suggestions in the chapters ahead, you can have faith that you will find ways to improve your sleep significantly and permanently.

2

Insomnia

Betty dreads crawling into bed each night. She's tried counting sheep and imagining ocean waves, only to find that her mind wanders back to the anxieties of the day. She struggles for a good hour in bed, but sleep eludes her. She looks at the clock repeatedly, a brightly lit digital thing, and it constantly reminds her in glaring detail how much time has passed. This, of course, only makes her more anxious. She says things to herself like, "If I don't go to sleep NOW I will NEVER be able to make it through tomorrow." Betty suffers from the most common type of insomnia, *sleep onset insomnia*.

Helen, on the other hand, falls asleep quickly. But after a couple of hours she becomes restless and wakes up. If she falls back asleep, she wakes up again, two or three times throughout the night. On some nights she cannot force herself to go back to sleep at all, and so spends the next day haggard and cranky. Helen is suffering from *sleep maintenance insomnia*, the second most common type of insomnia.

Eric is out the moment his head hits the pillow. His sleeping companion assures him he's snoring LOUDLY in seconds. But there he is, awake for the day at 4 a.m., mind racing. Eric suffers from *early morning awakening*, a third type of insomnia. All his thoughts, no matter how trivial they look in daylight, seem absolutely catastrophic in the wee hours.

People with sleep onset insomnia generally take longer than 30 minutes, at least three or more times per week, to fall asleep.

They experience a great deal of anxiety, obsessive thinking, and tossing and turning in trying to get to sleep. Sleep maintenance insomnia means that you probably fall asleep relatively easily, but wake up after a while, and then have trouble falling back to sleep. Obsessive thinking and anxiety can also characterize this type of problem, making it even more difficult to relax enough to return to sleep. Finally, there is some link to depression, stress and alcohol abuse with early morning awakening, or waking up hours before your scheduled rising time.

You may share some or all of these characteristics. Most insomniacs do not fit neatly into any of these specific categories, but exhibit a wide variety of tendencies based on age, personality, and sleep requirements. Although these designations have been used for many years, most clinicians are finding that the characteristics blend into each other. For example, you may require more, or less sleep than other people. Some "short sleepers" experience no disruption in functioning after only four hours of sleep, while others may feel exhausted after nine. Perhaps a better way to think about your insomnia is to categorize it as simply "transient" or "persistent." *Transient insomnia* is occasional and usually due to stress. You may be going through a particularly difficult time in your life, and experience bouts of poor quality sleep. You can probably identify an event or events that triggered your anxious reaction. As the stress subsides, so does the insomnia.

When you experience poor sleep over a longer period, at least two to three months, you may have developed *persistent insomnia.* Your sleep problem may have started out as transient insomnia, but due to negative conditioning it developed into a longer-term problem. You need to take care that your persistent insomnia does not involve a medical condition, such as sleep apnea. Refer to Chapter 4, *Sleep Disorders,* for more information about physical disorders and sleep. Chapter 3, which discusses conditioning and habit regulation, will also be useful.

The following widely used, multifaceted guidelines can help you identify insomnia. If nearly all the conditions match your experience, you suffer persistent insomnia. Any one symptom, however, can indicate sleep problems significant enough to disrupt functioning and warrant your attention.

1. Taking more than 30 minutes to fall asleep;
2. Being awake more than a total of 30 minutes during the night, or
3. Sleeping less than a total of six and one-half hours;
4. Experiencing daytime fatigue with decreased performance ability and increased moodiness;
5. Symptoms occurring three or more nights per week;
6. Symptoms persisting at least several months.

There are many social and psychological factors contributing to insomnia. Kales and Kales in their book *Evaluation and Treatment of Insomnia* list 18 factors that may contribute to chronic, or persistent, insomnia. The following is a condensed diagram of some of these factors:

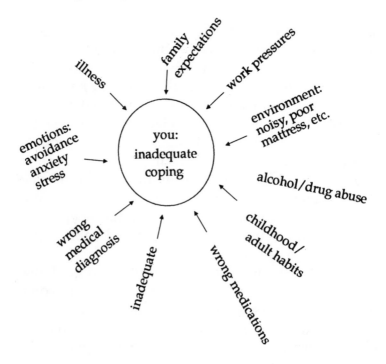

In the center of the diagram is "inadequate coping." Coping encompasses physical as well as emotional adjustment. Your probably already know that being physically tense hinders your ability to relax enough to go to sleep. Insomniacs are known to be people with a history of general physical arousal, meaning that they tense up easily and stay tensed for prolonged periods. This may mean higher muscle tension and blood pressure, faster heart rate, and poorer peripheral circulation. To make matters worse, all of these tendencies are exacerbated when you are under stress, creating a vicious cycle of anxiety—sleeplessness—more anxiety. If you know that you are the type of person who easily tenses up—your muscles are sore from tension and fatigue or you are prone to headaches—you will likely benefit from the relaxation exercises presented in

Chapter 6. Most insomniacs respond best, however, to a combination of relaxation exercises and cognitive control of their obsessional thinking.

Eight Psycho-Physiological Factors Involved in Insomnia

It is impossible to list factors shared by all insomniacs; the group is enormous and diverse, and the problem is unique for each individual. Nevertheless, some general tendencies link insomniacs. The fact that these characteristics are both psychological and physiological says something about the strong connection between thought patterns and physical responses.

Insomniacs as a group tend to have certain emotional characteristics that keep them from sleep. One primary characteristic is "fear of letting go." Insomniacs have trouble letting go not only of physical tension but also of thoughts. Do you find that you have difficulty accepting that a problem is not solvable? Can you say to yourself, "Let it go," and believe it? Your inability to let thoughts and feelings go leads to "obsessional thinking." You may catch yourself lying in bed at night obsessing about everything from potential personal failures to solving the world's problems. You may often feel a great deal of anger at yourself and others, and insecurity, and then blame yourself for not being perfect. These perfectionistic tendencies create destructive, circular patterns: you get angry, place blame, can't get to sleep, and then get angry with yourself for being so weak that you can't get to sleep. In summary, the eight typical characteristics are:

1. High physical arousal levels
2. Fear of letting go

3. Obsessional thinking
4. Fear of failure
5. Anger
6. Catastrophic thinking
7. Perfectionistic tendencies
8. Participation in vicious cycle patterns

If any or all of these eight thought and behavior patterns sound familiar, take heart. There are ways to counteract their negative effects, which interfere with your sleep. Chapters 6 and 7 will describe relaxation techniques you can use to calm your tense body. Chapter 8 goes into greater detail about specific techniques to manage your obsessive thinking and counteract that negative energy which only makes it harder for you to cope.

Aging and Insomnia

One factor not on the diagram or in the above list is aging. Aging is a fact of life, of course, and it has definite effects on sleep quality.

Human need for sleep changes with age. Newborn babies sleep about two-thirds of the time, decreasing to about 50%, or 12 hours per night, at six months of age. Children continue to sleep about 10 to 12 hours per night, leveling off at 7 ½ hours per night with teenagers and adults. By age 55, the hours of sleep increase to 8 or more again, but the sleep quality is different. Aged sleep tends to be lighter and more restless, with a typical number of awakenings at five per night. This can be a natural function of age, but it frightens some people into thinking they are suffering from insomnia. More information about aging and sleep appears in Chapter 13.

Summary

It's lonely being an insomniac. No one else—no doctor, parent, friend, or even spouse—can give you a magic cure to help you sleep. A cure, that is, that is healthy, practical, inexpensive, and non-addictive. What's worse, you face most of those feelings of isolation and frustration in the middle of the night, when others are snoozing peacefully. That's when you're likely to feel most resentful of others' ability to sleep. That's also when you probably obsess about all the things you think you're doing wrong in your life. You might even be tempted to lash out angrily at others and—directly or indirectly—blame them for your insomnia. You may wish or even insist that your significant other wake to share your misery. Resist this temptation; a friend doesn't need to share sleepless nights to sympathize with you. Chances are he or she already feels helpless and anxious about your condition.

This book is designed as a self-help guide to treatment. The exercises and ideas presented in these pages can help you identify and gain control over your sleep problems.

Nevertheless, it is often advisable to have yourself evaluated by a certified professional in a sleep lab. In part, this is to ensure that you are not overlooking a serious health problem. A professional evaluation also offers you an individualized, detailed profile of your condition. Please refer to Chapter 14, *Sleep and Chronic Pain,* for a description and discussion of the sleep lab experience.

3

Sleep Hygiene

In your quest to unravel your sleep problem, you may unknowingly overlook the obvious. Sometimes sleep problems are not related to complex physical or mental disorders, but are simply the result of poor habits. However, before you decide that your sleep problem fits into the category of "simple," it's a good idea to consult a sleep expert. As you will see in the next chapter, *Sleep Disorders*, certain sleep problems are serious enough to require immediate medical attention. You'll want to consult a sleep expert, or at least your family doctor, if you have any suspicion of a physical disorder.

Once a physical disorder is ruled out, it's time to consider your sleep hygiene, or sleep habits. Sometimes the simplest things can get in the way of good sleep. Throughout this chapter, scrutinize the habits you keep surrounding your uptimes and downtimes to see which ones may need altering. The first part of this chapter will help consider your personal habits such as diet, exercise, and time scheduling. In the second part, you can examine possible environmental factors that might significantly affect sleep quality, such as noise. A sample sleep diary is included at the end of this chapter; making copies and filling them in regularly can help you isolate significant factors and monitor your progress. Also, don't forget to take the sleep hygiene test at the end of the chapter.

Diet

Caffeine. One obvious food substance to avoid is caffeine. You probably know someone who brags about drinking coffee all day, and then sleeping soundly all night. Chances are, that person's sleep is affected more than he or she realizes. Caffeine is a powerful stimulant; most people will recognize the uncomfortable shakiness and general arousal of even small amounts of caffeine. In large doses, it can cause sweating, heart-racing, numbness, breathing difficulties, and paranoid feelings. Caffeine is a drug; you can develop a tolerance, but it will always act as a stimulant. Ingesting anything with caffeine in it even several hours before bedtime can cause difficulty falling asleep and fitful sleep long into the night. Do not drink caffeinated beverages after 4 p.m., or within six hours of your bedtime. If you can cut it out entirely, so much the better. Remember to check the labels on colas, teas, and some other drinks that may contain more caffeine than you realize. Some medications and foods, such as chocolate, contain caffeine. Take the sleep hygiene questionnaire at the end of this chapter to test your knowledge of caffeinated substances.

Nicotine. Like caffeine, nicotine is also a powerful stimulant. Sleep lab studies show that smokers averaging one and one-half packs a day take longer to fall asleep than non-smokers. Smokers also tend to experience more fitful sleep, which can be worsened by smoker's cough. The health hazards of smoking are well known, and insomnia sufferers should seriously consider giving up their smoking habit for reasons besides improved sleep. If this is simply not an option right now, try not to smoke within two to three hours of your bedtime.

Be aware that abrupt withdrawal of these central nervous system stimulants can have adverse affects. Some people experience headaches, restlessness, and feelings of panic and anxiety. The effects of caffeine withdrawal—headaches and irritability—may last as long as a week. Nicotine withdrawal can be much more intense. You need to plan carefully to quit smoking by consulting one of the many books available on the subject, or by checking with your health care professional.

Alcohol. One mythical sleep enhancer is alcohol. You might think of a hot toddy or a nightcap before retiring as relaxing. And they can be—at first. But alcohol taken in larger amounts before bedtime significantly disturbs your ability to maintain sleep. It also contributes to early morning awakening. Some individuals find that even smaller amounts of alcohol have a damaging effect on their sleep. If you are drinking heavily before bedtime in order to numb yourself to sleep or in an attempt to avoid obsessional thinking, you'll find that alcohol only makes matters worse. This has to do with alcohol's disruption of your natural sleep cycles. Researchers have demonstrated that alcohol initially decreases wakefulness, but—as it leaves your body—increases wakefulness in the last half of the night. You may fall asleep quickly, but you'll experience restlessness and fitful sleep later on in the night. The moral is not to use alcohol to sedate yourself to sleep.

Mealtimes. Mealtimes can be scheduled to reprogram your body to feel sleepy. Eat at regular times, and you will get into a routine which can help signal sleep time. If you eat a heavy meal before bedtime, you may find it difficult to relax enough to go to sleep, since your digestive system has to work overtime. For this reason, you'll want to have dinner at least three or four hours before retiring. Space your other meals out at regular intervals, leaving enough time for you to be hungry for an early dinner. If you need a snack before bedtime, drink warm milk. Or, try a light combination of carbohydrate and protein, such as bread and cheese or milk and crackers.

There is no specific food or drink that has been proven to promote sleep. However, some studies have demonstrated the beneficial effects of L-Tryptophan, an amino acid found in such common foods as meat, dairy products, beans and leafy green vegetables. Until recently, supplemental doses of L-Tryptophan were advised for those suffering from insomnia. The thought was that the amount of L-Tryptophan found in common foods was too small to have a significant effect on your sleep. However, recent reports indicate that large amounts of L-Tryptophan taken separately can pose serious health hazards. Since no one is known to have suffered from an old-fashioned glass of warm milk, it may be best to trust mom's advice and return to this natural source of the drug. Consult a doctor for the latest findings before partaking of any L-Tryptophan supplements.

Rigid weight loss plans can have an understandably negative effect on sleep quality. You may wake up in the middle of the night with hunger pangs. Try to space out your caloric intake throughout the day, so that you are able to consume some calories before bedtime to get you through the night.

Exercise

Exercise can be a key to helping you sleep better. Regular exercise has many benefits, psychological and emotional as well as physical. True, it can be hard to overcome inertia and get yourself started. But, the good news is that just a little exercise—taking a walk or gardening—can help alleviate depression, raise self-esteem, and promote a sense of well-being, all of which can benefit sleep. Regular exercise is habit-forming, and a fine replacement for the many less-healthy addictions you may struggle to break. Studies of the effects of an aerobic exercise regimen show that exercisers tend to have lower blood pressure, anxiety, and muscle tension, and are able to cope better with stress than non-exercisers. Studies also show that even simple regular exercise—stretching, strengthening, and gentle movements—helps people sleep better compared to those who are completely sedentary. This may be because exercise promotes the release of the chemical serotonin in your brain—neuro-transmitter thought to be connected to feelings of well-being and satisfaction. But the key word here is *regular*. Sporadic bursts of strenuous exercise may prove more painful than helpful. There is one other caveat about exercise: *avoid* exercise just before bedtime. Moderate or strenuous exercise has an initially arousing effect, making it difficult for you to relax. Many studies suggest that the best time of day to exercise is in the afternoon or early evening. Leave yourself about three to four hours between exercising and bedtime. That gives your body time to enjoy an athletic high, unwind slowly, and begin to want to rest.

The American College of Sports Medicine recommends that you spend 15 to 60 minutes, three to five days per week, doing some sort of aerobic exercise. Examples of appropriate aerobic exercises are running, brisk walking, swimming, cycling, rowing, aerobic dancing, cross-country skiing, and rope skipping. If you are over 45 and/or have heart disease risk factors, it's best to consult your health care professional before embarking on an aerobic exercise program.

Time Scheduling and Other Behaviors

The import regular uptimes, downtimes, and mealtimes has already been mentioned in the section "Diet Do's and Don'ts."

It bears repeating, however, that following a *regular schedule* can help "cue" your sleep urge. In an attempt to compensate for poor sleep, many insomniacs go to bed too early and try to force sleep. Or, they sleep late in the morning and take long naps. It is important for you to go to bed ONLY when you are sleepy. In addition, make yourself get up at the same time every morning: weekday and weekend, if you can. And, as you'll see below, it's essential that you skip naps. A major exception to this is older people who may benefit from regular napping; see the section on naps below, and Chapter 13 *Aging and Sleep.* In general, insomniacs need to re-regulate their timing systems and synchronize their internal clocks as closely as possible with the 24-hour day. For more information about biological rhythms, see Chapter 11.

Following a routine pre-bed ritual can help cue sleepiness, such as turning on a certain light in the bedroom at the same time each night. You might leave a not-too-exciting book or novel on your bedtable and read a chapter each night. Or rearrange your pillows in a certain way.

Avoid arousing, non-sleep enhancing activities just before bedtime, such as eating, watching an exciting movie, or anything else that gets your juices flowing. An exception is sexual activity, which tends to be relaxing for most people. If, however, you are a person who does not find sex satisfying (for example, a woman who does not have orgasms) you may want to consult a health care professional for counseling. Emotional distress in the form of sexual difficulty is a major contributor to insomnia, and should not be overlooked when trying to unravel a sleep problem.

To learn more about manipulating your daily activities to enhance sleep cues, see Chapter 9, *Conditioning Insomnia.*

Naps

As a general rule, insomniacs would be wise to avoid napping. Naps reinforce your poor nighttime sleep routine. There are some exceptions, however.

Naps may be beneficial for older people whose sleep patterns are shorter and lighter, leading to less overall sleep and more restless sleep. Even in this case, much of napping's benefit depends on the time of day the nap is taken. This relates to your body's circadian rhythm, which varies greatly with each individual. (Please refer to Chapter 11 for information on circadian rhythms). A 10 to 20 minute nap may refresh you midday, without affecting your nighttime sleepiness. Experiment to find the best time for such a catnap, if you find it helpful. If you work odd hours, you may also find yourself in need of a refresher or a break between different activities. But in general, *naps should not be used to replace lost and broken sleep.* Studies show that napping cannot substitute for a solid night of good sleep.

Don't let yourself use naps to avoid certain tasks or to compensate for feelings of despair and depression. If you have an underlying problem such as depression, naps can often be draining instead of refreshing. They also do little to help solve your problem—the depression, the unpleasant tasks, or the insomnia. Work on staying up during the day, and you'll be more likely to sleep during the night.

Environmental Factors to Consider

Noise. If you suspect that you are particularly sensitive to noise, take stock of the noise situation in your bedroom. One researcher, Dr. Patricia Lacks of Washington University in St. Louis, Mo., has found that sensitivity to noise increases as people age, and that women seem more sensitive to noise than men. If you have noisy neighbors or live near an airport or freeway—and moving is not an option—look into soundproofing your bedroom. This can be done by adding insulation or special building materials to the walls. Healthy, satisfying sleep is worth the added expense. A cheaper alternative is to experiment with various types of "white noise," such as fans, air conditioners, or audio tapes of ocean waves. Or inquire about the latest in ear plugs: fiberglass.

If you are disturbed or awakened by too much light in your bedroom, experiment with different types of eye shades, window shades, and light blocking curtains. If the blackness of the night makes you uneasy, buy a nightlight and plug it in where you can see it easily.

Don't forget to appraise the quality of your mattress. Is it too firm or too soft? I once complained of annoying hip pain for weeks until I slept on a very firm mattress, and the pain disappeared.

Room Temperature. Another researcher, Dr. Peter Huri, found that when room temperature rises above 75 degrees F, people wake up more often, experience more restless sleep and less dreaming sleep, and sleep less deeply. The opposite extreme also presents problems: if the room is too cold, you're probably unable to fall asleep. Optimum temperatures range somewhere between 65 and 70 degrees F.

Clocks. Get rid of pre-set hourly watch beepers or chimers, if they disturb your sleep even in the slightest amount. While some people can tune out external noise such as a chiming clock, others may find that the hourly gong only reinforces their obsessional characteristics by reminding them of each passing hour. If you find yourself counting each hour that passes and anticipating the next chime, indicating another sleepless hour, then turn it off.

Bedmates. The presence or absence of a bed partner can be a significant sleep factor. A restless bedmate or a loud snorer is likely to disturb your sleep. You might try earplugs, a mattress specially designed to minimize bouncing, or even separate beds if the problem warrants. Of course, you'll want to help your bedmate solve his or her sleep problems; remember, snoring can denote a more profound medical problem. At the other extreme, if you are accustomed to your bedmate, you may find it hard to sleep well without him or her. Time alone may help you, as well as some of the relaxation techniques discussed in later chapters.

In summary, sensible sleep hygiene is a matter of common sense. Pay attention to your routine, diet, exercise, and environment. Test your knowledge and evaluate your sleep hygiene by taking a few minutes to fill out the following questionnaire.

Using a Sleep Diary

You can use the following sleep diary to monitor your sleep progress. Daily and diligent use of a sleep diary can provide you with an overall picture of your sleep patterns and habits. Do not be concerned with answering the questions perfectly. For example, estimate the number of minutes it generally took you to fall asleep, rather than obsess about getting all the minutes recorded exactly right.

This tool is intended to reinforce positive behaviors by providing you with a subjective assessment. On the bottom of each day's entry record any information that you feel affects the quality of sleep, such as a particular relaxation exercise you are trying or the amount of exercise you got that day. Don't forget to include the amount of medications, alcohol, or nicotine used, if applicable.

You will want to continue to fill in your sleep diary for at least two to three weeks. The responses from the right-hand column can be compared over time for a general view of your progress; the left-hand column lets you focus specifically on each night's experience.

Daily Sleep Diary

Date:_____

1. A. Time I went to bed: ___:___

    B. Time I fell asleep: ___:___
        (Last time I saw on clock)

*Approximate time
to fall asleep:
_____ minutes*

2. A. How many times I woke
        up during the night: _____

    B. How long I stayed awake
        during each uptime: _____

                                     _____

                                     _____

                                     _____

    C. Time I woke up for the day:_____

*Approximate total
time sleeping:
_____hours
_____minutes*

3. A. How easy was it to fall asleep
        last night?

          1   2   3   4   5
        (very hard)   (very easy)

    B. How rested did I feel this morning?

          1   2   3   4   5
        (very tired)   (very rested)

C. What quality sleep did I experience last night?

    1   2   3   4   5
(very poor)   (very good)

D. How free of physical tension was I when I went to bed?

    1   2   3   4   5
(very tense)   (tension-free)

E. How free of mental activity (planning, thinking,
    worrying) was I when I went to bed?

    1   2   3   4   5
(mind racing)   (mind quiet)

F. How well am I functioning today?

    1   2   3   4   5
(very poorly)   (very well)   *On a scale of 6 (poor
                                                  sleep) to 30 (excellent
                                                  sleep), last night
                                                  rates_____ (Add
                                                  responses A - F)*

4. Additional notes:

Aerobic exercise—when:_____ effect: positive negative unsure

		positive	negative	unsure
Relaxation exercise	_____	+	-	?
Stretching exercise	_____	+	-	?
Evening snack (what:_____)	_____	+	-	?
Last alcoholic beverage (total # of drinks:_____)	_____	+	-	?
Last cigarette (total smoked:_____)	_____	+	-	?
Sleeping pills (kind:_____)	_____	+	-	?

Special circumstances or experiences:_____

Owl and Lark Questionnaire

Adapted from "A Self-Assessment Questionnaire to Determine Morningness-Eveningness in Human Circadian Rhythms," by J.A. Horne and O. Ostberg. *International Journal of Chronobiology*, Vol. 4. 97-110, 1976. As printed in *Wide Awake at 3:00 A.M.*, by Richard Coleman. W.H. Freeman and Co. (New York: 1986).

Are you a morning person or an evening person? The answer can tell you a great deal about your body's natural rhythms. If you're a strong morning type—a lark—you probably peak a short time after waking up, and fade slowly as the day progresses. Strong evening types—owls—don't peak until late in the day or evening, and take a long time to awaken fully as the day begins. Owls also have an easier time adjusting to changes in schedule or time zone than strong morning types; larks find such changes very difficult. Most people fall somewhere between the two extremes, as "moderately morning types," "moderately evening types," or even "neithers." They can modify their sleep-wake cycles to adapt to weekends, shift work, or new time zones with only moderate difficulty.

You probably have some idea where you belong on the spectrum. Still, the questionnaire results may surprise you. Be honest in your answers, and let your first reactions stand. After you've marked the most appropriate box under each question, tally your score by adding the numbers under the boxes you chose. Identify your type as follows:

	Score
Strong Morning Type	70-86
Moderately Morning Type	59-69
Neither Type	42-58
Moderately Evening Type	31-41
Strong Evening Type	16-30

1. Considering only your own "feeling best" rhythm, at what time would you get up if you were entirely free to plan your day?

Before 6:00 a.m. . . . . □ 5
6:00 - 7:00 a.m. . . . . □ 4
7:00 - 9:00 a.m. . . . . □ 3
9:00 - 10:00 a.m. . . . . □ 2
After 10:00 a.m. . . . . □ 1

2. Considering only your own "feeling best" rhythm, at what time would you go to bed if you were entirely free to plan your evening?

Before 9:00 p.m. . . . . □ 5
9:00 - 10:00 p.m. . . . . □ 4
10:00 - 12:00 a.m. . . . . □ 3
12:00 - 1:00 a.m. . . . . □ 2
After 1:00 a.m. . . . . □ 1

3. If there is a specific time at which you have to get up in the morning, to what extent are you dependent on being woken up by an alarm clock?

Not at all dependent . . . . □ 4
Slightly dependent . . . . □ 3
Fairly dependent . . . . □ 2
Very dependent . . . . □ 1

4. Assuming adequate environmental conditions, how easy do you find getting up in the mornings?

Not at all easy . . . . □ 1
Not very easy . . . . □ 2
Fairly easy . . . . □ 3
Very easy . . . . □ 4

5. How alert do you feel during the first half hour after having woken in the mornings?

Not at all alert . . . . □ 1
Slightly alert . . . . □ 2
Fairly alert . . . . □ 3
Very alert . . . . □ 4

6. How is your appetite during the first half-hour after having woken in the mornings?

Very poor . . . . □ 1
Fairly poor . . . . □ 2
Fairly good . . . . □ 3
Very good . . . . □ 4

7. During the first half-hour after having woken in the morning, how tired do you feel?

Very tired . . . . □ 1
Fairly tired . . . . □ 2
Fairly refreshed . . . . □ 3
Very refreshed . . . . □ 4

8. When you have no commitments the next day, at what time do you go to bed compared to your usual bedtime?

Seldom or never later . . . . □ 4
Less than one hour later . . . . □ 3
1-2 hours later . . . . □ 2
More than two hours later . . . . . . □ 1

9. You have decided to engage in some physical exercise. A friend suggests that you do this one hour twice a week and the best time for him is between 7:00 - 8:00 a.m. Bearing in mind nothing else but your own "feeling best" rhythm how do you think you would perform?

Would be in good form .... ☐ 4
Would be in reasonable form ..... ☐ 3
Would find it difficult .... ☐ 2
Would find it very difficult ...... ☐ 1

10. At what time in the evening do you feel tired and as a result in need of sleep?

Before 9:00 p.m. .... ☐ 5
9:00 - 10:00 p.m. .... ☐ 4
10:00 - 12:00 a.m................. ☐ 3
12:00 - 1:00 a.m.................. ☐ 2
After 1:00 a.m................... ☐ 1

11. You wish to be at your peak performance for a test which you know is going to be mentally exhausting and lasting for two hours. You are entirely free to plan your day considering only your own "feeling best" rhythm which ONE of the four testing times would you choose?

8:00 - 10:00 a.m.................. ☐ 6
11:00 a.m. - 1:00 p.m. .... ☐ 4
3:00 - 5:00 p.m. .... ☐ 2
7:00 - 9:00 p.m. .... ☐ 0

12. If you went to bed at 11:00 p.m. at what level of tiredness would you be?

Not at all tired .... ☐ 0
A little tired .... ☐ 2
Fairly tired .... ☐ 3
Very tired .... ☐ 5

13. For some reason you have gone to bed several hours later than usual, but there is no need to get up at any particular time the next morning. Which ONE of the following events are you most likely to experience?

Will wake up at usual time and will NOT fall asleep .... ☐ 4
Will wake up at usual time and will doze thereafter .... ☐ 3
Will wake up at usual time but will fall asleep again .... ☐ 2
Will NOT wake up until later than usual .... ☐ 1

14. One night you have to remain awake between 4:00 and 6:00 a.m. in order to carry out night watch. You have no commitments the next day. Which ONE of the following alternatives will suit you best?

Would NOT go to bed until watch was over .... ☐ 1
Would take a nap before and sleep after .... ☐ 2
Would take a good sleep before and nap after .... ☐ 3
Would take ALL sleep before watch .... ☐ 4

15. You have to do two hours of hard physical work. You are entirely free to plan your day and considering only your own "feeling best" rhythm which ONE of the following times would you choose?

8:00 - 10:00 a.m. . . . . □ 4
11:00 AM - 1:00 p.m. . . . . □ 3
3:00 - 5:00 p.m. . . . . □ 2
7:00 - 9:00 p.m. . . . . □ 1

16. You have decided to engage in hard physical exercise. A friend suggests that you do this for one hour twice a week and the best time for him is between 10:00 - 11:00 p.m. Bearing in mind nothing else but your own "feeling best" rhythm how well do you think you would perform?

Would be in good form . . . . □ 1
Would be in reasonable form . . . . . □ 2
Would find it difficult . . . . □ 3
Would find it very difficult . . . . . . □ 4

17. Suppose that you can choose your own work hours. Assume that you worked a FIVE-hour day (including breaks) and that your job was interesting and paid by results. Which FIVE CONSECUTIVE HOURS would you select?

4:00 - 9:00 a.m. . . . . □ 5
7:00 - noon . . . . □ 4
10:00 - 3:00 p.m. . . . . □ 3
4:00 - 9:00 p.m. . . . . □ 2
9:00 p.m. - 1:00 a.m. . . . . □ 1

18. At what time of the day do you think that you reach your "feeling best" peak?

5:00 - 7:00 a.m. . . . . □ 5
8:00 - 9:00 a.m. . . . . □ 4
10:00 a.m. - 4:00 p.m. . . . . □ 3
5:00 p.m. - 9:00 p.m. . . . . □ 2
10:00 p.m. - 4:00 a.m. . . . . □ 1

19. One hears about "morning" and "evening" types of people. Which ONE of these types do you consider yourself to be?

Definitely a "morning" type . . . . . . □ 6
Rather more a "morning" than
an "evening" type . . . . □ 4
Rather more an "evening" than
a "morning" type . . . . □ 2
Definitely an "evening" type . . . . . □ 0

Further Reading

Anch, Michael A.; Carl P. Browman; Merrill M. Mitler; James K. Walsh. *Sleep: A Scientific Perspective.* Englewood Cliffs, New Jersey: Prentice Hall, 1988.

Hauri, Peter. *The Sleep Disorders.* Kalamazoo, Mi.: Upjohn, 1982.

Lacks, Patricia. *Behavioral Treatment For Persistent Insomnia.* New York: Pergamon Press, 1987.

4

Sleep Disorders

Most poor sleepers can learn to manage insomnia through behavioral techniques such as proper sleep hygiene and relaxation. But some forms of insomnia have underlying physical disorders which may require careful medical attention. These disorders can be mere annoyances, as with occasional teeth grinding, or life threatening, as with sleep apnea.

Before you decide that you definitely do or do not suffer from one of the disorders described in this chapter, it can be a good idea to have yourself evaluated at a qualified sleep center. Sleep apnea and narcolepsy are serious enough to require professional consultation; sleep specialists will be able to provide you with appropriate diagnosis, treatment, and medication. This chapter is intended to give you a brief but comprehensive overview of the most common physical disorders affecting sleep quality.

First is the most life threatening sleep disorder, *sleep* apnea, also known as the "snoring sickness." This is the most common of all organic sleep disorders, and appears in the first section. Following are nocturnal *myoclonus,* or intermittent leg twitching and jerking throughout the night, and *restless leg syndrome,* severe leg "aches" that inhibit sleep onset. Both of these disorders, occurring in only a small percentage of the adult population, are described in the second section. Last is *narcolepsy,* or excessive daytime sleepiness. This is the least common of all organic sleep disorders, but it can be extremely life disruptive.

A fourth category of disorder is termed *parasomnias,* or disorders of partial arousal. While the disorders previously mentioned are believed to have a strong organic component, the parasomnias are more behaviorally based and occur for the most part in childhood. A small percentage of the adult population does experience parasomnias, however. The most commonly acknowledged parasomnias are sleep walking (or *somnabulism*), night terrors, nightmares and teeth grinding (or *bruxism*). The other most commonly recognized parasomnia is *nocturnal enuresis,* or bedwetting, which is not covered in this book. For a discussion of parasomnias, please refer to Chapter 12, *Sleep and Dreaming.*

While sleep apnea, narcolepsy, and restless legs have little in common symptomatically, they do share two similarities: they have an underlying physical cause, and they significantly reduce your sleep and life quality. Don't hesitate to seek adequate professional help for these troublesome and threatening disorders.

Sleep Apnea—The Snoring Sickness

It has long been a myth that loud snoring signifies a sound sleeper. Snoring, however, is now known to signal a potentially life threatening disorder: sleep apnea. Most people suffering from sleep apnea are unaware of its disruptive symptoms throughout the night. They wake up feeling unrefreshed and struggle through the day in a fatigued state, yet are unaware that they probably woke up hundreds of times throughout the night gasping for air. Often it is the bedmate who alerts sleep experts of the loud choking, gasping, and nonstop snoring sounds of the sleep apnea sufferer.

Sleep apnea sufferers generally breathe normally during the day, but their breathing becomes shallow at night. At times it ceases altogether for a few seconds and up to two minutes. This can cause partial or complete arousal from sleep and may go on all night. Males seem to develop this condition more often than females, and there is evidence that it appears more frequently in the elderly. Other factors that may play a part in contributing to sleep apnea are obesity and short, thick necks. Those who have narcolepsy tend to develop sleep apnea more often than the population as a whole. The only way to make a definite diagnosis of this condition is to be evaluated overnight in a sleep lab.

Experts describe three types of sleep apnea:

Central Sleep Apnea is relatively rare and found in those whose chief complaints are insomnia and excessive sleepiness. Central sleep apnea is thought to originate in the brain, which sends a message to the diaphragm to stop moving in and out with air intake and exhalation, causing breathing to stop altogether.

Obstructive Sleep Apnea, also known as "upper airway sleep apnea," is more common than central sleep apnea. In this condition, the diaphragm is not involved. Muscles of the upper airway (tongue, throat and pharynx) relax so significantly that the throat collapses and breathing is completely blocked.

Mixed Sleep Apnea is a combination of the above two conditions and is seen only occasionally.

The American Medical Association lists the following additional symptoms likely to appear as the disorder worsens:

1. *Unusual body movements* such as wildly kicking arms and legs;
2. *Sleepwalking,* which may involve the person simply sitting up in bed in order to get more air;
3. *Blackouts or episodes of automatic behavior* which occur during waking hours. These episodes may last several minutes to hours and involve the person repeating tasks in a robot-like fashion. Sufferers may seem incoherent during a conversation. This behavior is similar to a narcoleptic attack described in the third section.
4. *Intellectual fogginess* or inability to concentrate and a feeling of disorientation;
5. *Hallucinations or bizarre illusions* similar to dreaming;
6. *Personality changes* such as depression, irritability and anxiety;
7. *Loss of interest in sex* affecting both sexes. Men may find it difficult to have or to keep an erection;
8. *Morning Headaches* and confusion upon awakening;
9. *Bed-wetting.*

Treatment

The most frequently and successfully used method of treatment for sleep apnea is "C-PAP," or Continuous

Positive Airway Pressure. This mechanical device can be rented from home health care companies and consists of a portable generator, a tube, and a mask. The device gently blows air into your mouth and nose to prevent collapse of the upper airway muscles and eliminate snoring. It makes only a light noise which is not disruptive to you or your bedmate.

Doctors can prescribe certain medications such as protriptilyne and progesterone, to stimulate breathing. In addition, they will encourage the sleep apnea sufferer to lose weight, stop smoking (which irritates the upper airway), avoid alcohol, use a vaporizer to keep airways clear of congestion, and use pillows to elevate the head. Some devices are recommended, such as mouthguards, for obstructive sleep apnea. Simple corrective surgery may also be recommended, where the interior of the throat is enlarged. Or, for severe cases of sleep apnea—100 or more interruptions in breathing in six hours of sleep—a tracheostomy is performed. This relatively simple surgery involves inserting a tube into the windpipe, bypassing the throat area and allowing air to pass directly into the lungs. The tube is removed during the day to allow for a normal social life.

A word of caution. Unless carefully monitored and administered, drugs can be fatal to a sleep apnea sufferer. This condition puts a severe strain on the cardiac system due to constant awakenings. In addition, the sedating effects of alcohol, tranquilizers, and sleeping pills can further aggravate and depress the respiratory system. Be sure to check with your health care professional and/or a sleep lab expert to determine the appropriate kind and amount of medication.

Nocturnal Myoclonus

Sufferers of nocturnal myoclonus experience nightly muscle movements, usually in the legs and sometimes very violent. Typically they are not aware of these intermittent and rhythmic leg jerks and must rely on a bed partner to clue them in to their kicking and fitful sleep. Some people who have this unusual disorder are partially or completely awakened in the night and report fatigue and lethargy the next day. This disorder runs in families, becomes more frequent and severe with age, and must be confirmed by an evaluation in a sleep lab.

Treatment

The cause of nocturnal myoclonus is unknown. Treatment consists of regular exercise and a drugs used for seizure disorders which is called clonazepam.

Restless Leg Syndrome

Sometimes known as "nervous legs," this disorder is similar to nocturnal myoclonus in that its origin is unknown and sufferers experience leg jerks. However, it occurs mostly as the person is trying to fall asleep, making it difficult for him or her to relax enough to go to sleep. One patient describes this disorder as "uncomfortable but not painful sensations creeping deep inside the calf." Studies show that restless leg syndrome becomes more severe with age, sleep deprivation, and pregnancy.

Treatment

Moving about often relieves the discomfort. Also, an adequate exercise program combined with some form of muscle relaxaton has brought relief to some people with this disorder. Restless leg syndrome runs in families and may be due to poor circulation. Medications such as carbannazepine and clonidine have also been proven effective, but have not been adequately studied for conclusive results. Most people with restless leg syndrome also have nocturnal myoclonus.

Narcolepsy

People with narcolepsy are sometimes regarded as "lazy" and "incompetent" because they will suddenly and without apparent reason fall soundly asleep in the middle of daily activities such as eating, talking, even driving. Narcoleptics may not even be aware that they suffer from this devastating disease, only that they regularly experience chronic fatigue. Sometimes these mini-sleeps can be a mere annoyance, but they can be disastrous when they cause accidents or trouble holding down a job. Dr. William Dement of Stanford University reported in 1983 that in a study of narcolptics, 41 percent had occupational disabilities, 89 percent had deteriorating relationships, and 91 percent had accidents they attributed to their sleepiness. The exact physical mechanism causing narcolepsy is unknown, although it is thought to be a defect in central nervous system functioning.

Usually there is a family history of narcolepsy, with males and females equally affected. First signs routinely appear in the early teens and twenties, and symptoms worsen with age.

Another sign of narcolepsy is *excessive daytime sleepiness* (EDS), also often referred to as "sleep attacks." These attacks usually last 10 to 15 minutes, unless the person is lying or sitting, in which case sleep may last two to three hours. Narcoleptics often awake fully refreshed from these sleep attacks. However, their regular nighttime sleep is usually disturbed by multiple awakenings, temporary suspension of breathing (similar to sleep apnea—see the previous section), restlessness, nightmares, and disturbing images upon sleep onset and awakening, called hypnagogic hallucinations. Narcoleptics rarely feel fully alert and refreshed through the day, even after extended sleep.

About 60 percent of all narcoleptics experience *cataplexy,* a brief or sudden loss of muscle control. This muscle weakness can last several minutes and result in a physical collapse; the person experiences paralysis but remains fully or partially conscious. These attacks are usually triggered by emotions such as laughter, excitement, and anger. For this reason, some narcoleptics try not to respond emotionally and may in fact avoid situations likely to evoke strong emotions.

Narcoleptics typcially fall asleep in less than five minutes (compared to an average of 12 to 20 minutes for most adults to fall asleep) and go immediately into REM sleep. REM sleep, or rapid eye movement sleep, is the stage where most dreaming occurs, and the normal adult population moves into REM in about 90 minutes. This immediate intrusion of REM into the narcoleptic's sleep may account for the sometimes terrifying *hypnagogic hallucinations,* which occur right at the beginning and end of sleep. These hallucinations are vivid, dreamlike images which are not uncommon among most people. However, narcoleptics experience them immediately upon falling asleep, during a cataplectic episode and sometimes when fully conscious.

Sleep paralysis is sometimes a symptom of narcolepsy, where sufferers feel as if they cannot move a single muscle when falling asleep or waking up. This feeling can last for a few seconds or up to several minutes. Sleep paralysis combined with hypnagogic hallucinations is less frequent than the first two symptoms (EDS and cataplexy) but is terrifying nonetheless.

Harvey, an office worker, has had bouts of sleep paralysis since childhood. He remains fully conscious, but can't move a single muscle, except a finger. He has learned to wiggle that finger until he wakes up. "If I roll over right away and don't get up," he says, "I'll fall right back into that paralyzed state." Harvey, whose roots are in the Southeastern United States, has elderly relatives who call this condition having a "hag riding your back." Evidently the imaginary hag, or witch, needs to harass the sleeper. Southern folklore has it that if you leave a broom by your bed, the witch will be preoccupied counting the bristles and won't ride your back!

Treatment

Some success has been found treating narcolepsy with certain medications, such as a stimulant named ridilyn used to counteract excessive daytime sleepiness. Doctors also suggest scheduling naps at strategic times; narcoleptics are sometimes able to ward off sleep attacks by intentionally taking naps at certain times of the day. Intermittent use of napping and medications has been a helpful combination for some. Supportive counseling and the education of friends, family, co-workers, and bosses are also necessary additions to any treatment plan for narcolepsy. Sleep apnea and narcolepsy share a common symptom of excessive daytime sleepiness, but should not be confused, since their treatments are extremely different.

Drug Abuse and Sleep Disorders

If you have transient insomnia, your physician may recommend that you take hypnotic medication for a brief period of time. A typical drug might be Halcyon, which is described more thoroughly in the next chapter, on medications. Taking a time-limited course of sleeping pills will not lead to addiction, because with only a few nights of use, tolerance cannot be established. However, if your sleep problem becomes persistent, sleeping pills are not the answer and will exacerbate your sleep problem. Further, if you become addicted to sleep medication and then attempt to withdraw from it, you may experience a rebound effect of extreme sleeplessness, disturbed sleep, and nightmares. Check with your doctor about the appropriate use of sleeping pills, and read the next chapter carefully.

5

Medications for Sleep

By James K. Walsh, Ph.D.

The aim of this book is to help you find long-term relief—a cure—for insomnia. For this reason, the emphasis has been on behavioral treatment: changing your thoughts, habits, and attitudes surrounding sleep. For many people, behavioral changes are the surest way to achieve lasting and satisfying solutions to chronic sleep problems. No sleeping medication can cure insomnia.

Nevertheless, medications are sometimes useful. In case of transient insomnia (lasting a few days to a week), and short-term insomnia (lasting one to several weeks), appropriate medication can relieve the immediate stress of lost sleep, and prevent a temporary crisis from mushrooming into a more serious one. In some cases of chronic insomnia, medications can serve as temporary treatment to be used in conjunction with medical or behavioral options. While the insomnia won't improve until the underlying factors *causing* the insomnia are addressed, supervised pharmacological treatment can break the painful cycle of sleepless nights and anxious days. That can give you the energy and encouragement you need to combat the source of your sleep difficulties.

As you have read in the previous chapters, knowledge of the types of insomnia and the variety of possible causes has increased greatly during the past two decades. This knowledge has affected the way sleep medications are used in medical practice. More specific treatments are becoming available for some types of insomnia; more is known about some classes of drugs commonly prescribed. Most experts believe that pharmacological treatment for sleep disturbance can be helpful for certain patients when an appropriate evaluation has been undertaken. They also agree on some common caveats and precautions. This chapter will focus on the advantages and disadvantages of medications commonly used to promote sleep. Only a doctor can determine what medications—if any—are best for you. But knowing the options available will help you participate in the decision and weigh the risk and benefits.

Studies indicate that prescription sleeping pill use fell steadily over the 10-year period beginning in 1971. Yet, over 20 million prescriptions were written in 1981. Add to this the millions of individuals taking "nerve pills" or tranquilizers at bedtime, or using over-the-counter (OTC) sleep aids available without prescription, and you can see the continuing popularity of drug treatment.

Several different types of drugs are prescribed to improve sleep; others are used for this purpose even though they may be prescribed for other reasons. The most commonly prescribed drugs are the benzodiazepines (BZDs). Other prescription drugs include barbiturates and anti-depressants. Non-prescription, or OTC, drugs are often self-administered to combat sleep difficulty, as is alcohol. In some instances, illicit drugs are used for sleep induction (e.g., marijuana). In one sense, then, all of these can be considered "sleeping pills" or "sleeping medications." As you might guess, some are far less advisable than others.

All prescription sleeping medications alter the sleep stages which occur as you sleep. In general, these drugs decrease the stage one—light, transitional sleep— while increasing the stage two. At higher doses, REM sleep ("rapid eye movement," or dreaming sleep) and "slow-wave" sleep may also be suppressed. Although decreasing light sleep seems desirable, the significance of decreasing SWS or REM sleep is not fully understood. Some experts believe that slow wave sleep represents the "best" or "deepest," most restorative sleep. If REM is significantly suppressed by a drug, abrupt discontinuation typically leads to an increase in REM sleep. This "REM rebound" may be associated with vivid dreaming, possibly even nightmares. This same phenomenon occurs if REM is suppressed without medication. It suggests that REM sleep must be made up if lost. Nevertheless, no behavioral consequences have been noted even when REM is markedly reduced for weeks or months. REM rebound is not physically dangerous, but keep in mind that in some cases unpleasant, vivid dreams may occur.

Side Effects and Daytime Functioning

Most sleeping medications fall into the class of drugs known as sedative-hypnotics. Hypnotic medications reduce alertness and promote sleepiness. In cases of insomnia, this is usually a desired effect. However, this sedation can become a side effect (an undesired effect) with the passage of time. One type of side effect occurs when the sedating properties of a sleeping pill given at night continue into the waking hours. This can cause an individual to feel even worse during the daytime than he or she commonly feels following a night of disturbed sleep. More importantly, alertness and performance may be significantly impaired. The goal of treatment is to improve daytime functioning as well as sleep. Thus a sleeping medication that improves sleep significantly but results in daytime sleepiness or "morning hangover" has not met this goal. A sleeping pill with a long duration of action is much more likely to produce carry-over effects than one with a shorter duration of action, because the long-acting medication stays in the body for a longer period of time than the short-acting medication. Also, the higher the dose, the longer the medication will remain pharmacologically active, and the greater the likelihood of its interfering with daytime functioning.

Tolerance

Chronic use of sedative-hypnotics can in some cases lead to the development of tolerance to the medication. This means a previously effective amount of medication becomes ineffective over time, usually a period of weeks or months. As tolerance develops, the sleep disturbance returns, which may encourage the user to increase the dosage of medication. If this pattern is repeated often enough, it may result in drug dependency along with persistent sleep disturbance. Therefore, it is usually wise to limit nightly use of sleep medications to short periods of time, or to use them a few nights per week. The dose of the drug should not be increased, once an effective dose has been established.

Discontinuation Effects

Sleeping pills rarely "cure" the insomnia. That is, they do not very often correct whatever factors are leading to the insomnia. It should not be surprising, then, to learn that if the medication is stopped, the sleep disturbance returns. In some cases, discontinuation of sedative-hypnotic medication, particularly after high doses, may result in a few nights of sleep disturbance which is more severe than that present before treatment. This withdrawal effect often includes REM-rebound, and is termed "rebound insomnia." If the withdrawal effects are particularly severe, they may encourage return to use of medication. Avoiding dosages greater than the lowest effective dose will minimize the likelihood of "rebound insomnia."

Prescription Sleep Medications

The benzodiazepines (BZDs) are now the most commonly prescribed medication to promote sleep. In the United States, there are three benzodiazepines that currently have FDA approval for treatment of insomnia: flurazepam (Dalmane), temazepan (Restoril), and triazolam (Halcion). A number of others are marketed as anti-anxiety agents but are used as sleeping pills (see the table of BZDs, on the following page). Other BZDs and BZD-like compounds are under development. BZDs are recommended frequently because they are generally effective and have a larger safety margin than other sleep medications. Research studies have consistently demonstrated that BZDs reduce the time it takes for people to fall asleep, reduce the number and length of awakenings at night, and, as a result, increase total sleep time. These medications are considered safer than other types of sleep-promoting drugs because the doses of BZDs which are effective in improving sleep are much lower than the amount required to produce serious reactions such as breathing irregularity, coma, or death. Other types of medications (e.g., barbiturates) have a smaller margin between effective dose and the dose that produces serious reactions. Thus, overdosing on BZDs is much less likely than with other sleeping pills.

Benzodiazepines currently available in the United States

Generic or Chemical Name	Brand or Trade Name
alprazolam	Xanax
chlordiazepoxide	Librium
clorazepate	Tranxene
diazepam	Valium
flurazepam*	Dalmane
halazepam	Paxipam
lorazepam	Ativan
oxazepam	Serax
prazepam	Centrax
temazepam*	Restoril
triazolam*	Halcion

*These compounds have the approval of the Food and Drug Administration (FDA) for the treatment of insomnia.

Another reason that BZDs are relatively safe medications is that they do not interact with many other medications. That is, they will not influence the effectiveness or safety of most other medications a person may be taking for other health problems (although there are exceptions). In contrast, barbiturates and other non-BZD sedatives have a greater potential for changing the effects of other medications. This does not mean, however, that it is safe to drink alcohol or take certain prescription pain medications while taking BZDs. The sedating effects of BZDs will be intensified by alcohol and other central nervous system depressant drugs (e.g., codeine) and therefore these drugs should not be used in combination.

Even though BZDs are safer than other sleep medications, they must be approached with caution. Abrupt termination of long-term, very high-dosage BZD use has been shown to trigger serious, possibly life threatening symptoms such as seizures, high fever, panic reactions, hallucinations, and delusions. There have even been reports of some withdrawal symptoms after long-term use of moderate doses of BZDs, but there are no controlled studies to substantiate these reports. Because of differing sensitivities to drugs of this type, withdrawal from long-term or high dose BZD use should always be done under the supervision of a physician using gradual reductions in your dose so that symptoms can be minimized.

Anti-depressant drugs with sedative effects are occasionally prescribed for the treatment of insomnia in patients who are not depressed. Unfortunately, little objective research has examined the effects of these drugs in non-depressed insomnia patients. They are not as safe as BZDs in terms of overdose or drug interaction dangers. However, anti-depressants may have reduced likelihood of dependence or abuse compared to BZDs. Depressed individuals who take anti-depressants often experience improvement in their sleep. But the drug's primary effect is on the depression, not on the insomnia. Research has yet to determine the benefits—and drawbacks—of anti-depressants for non-depressed insomniacs.

Over-the-Counter Medications

Medications marketed as sleeping pills that are available without a doctor's prescription have not been shown by scientific studies to be effective in the treatment of insomnia. Most of these compounds contain one or more antihistamines as the sedating agent. In many individuals, antihistamines can produce drowsiness; however, there is little evidence that insomnia is significantly improved with such OTC medications.

L-tryptophan is an amino acid that has gained popularity as an OTC sleeping pill, although it has not been marketed for this sole purpose. Scientific investigations provide conflicting results concerning this substance, with some studies suggesting effective treatment of sleep disturbance and nearly as many suggesting no benefit. At the time that this chapter is being written, L-tryptophan is being investigated because of recent reports of eosinophilia associated with its use. Eosinophilia is an increase in a type of white blood cell that can affect several organ systems and, in extreme cases, can be fatal. The Food and Drug Administration is attempting to determine whether the cases of eosinophilia are due to L-tryptophan per se or if some of it became contaminated in the manufacturing or distribution process. Until the findings are conclusive, it's a good idea to avoid L-tryptophan supplements. The amino acid is present in natural form in many dairy products and other foods.

Alcohol

It is not uncommon for individuals to use alcohol as a sleep inducer. Because it is a potent central nervous system sedative, sleep onset is hastened. However, tolerance to this effect occurs fairly rapidly. What's more, though alcohol may help induce sleep, sleep in the latter portions of the night becomes disturbed. As the alcohol is metabolized, the sedative effect wears off and a marked arousal response occurs due to sympathetic nervous system activity. The result may range from shallow fragmented sleep, if alcohol consumption was moderate, to long periods of wakefulness after heavy drinking. The net effect is generally a less refreshing night of sleep. Tolerance, dependence, and discontinuation effects are also significant concerns when alcohol is used as a sleep aid. Tolerance to alcohol develops rapidly, often prompting the individual to drink a larger quantity for the desired sedating effect. Discontinuation of alcohol leads to profoundly disturbed sleep, which is likely to persist for several weeks to many months after alcohol is completely discontinued. Experts strongly advise not using alcohol to promote sleep.

Sleep Medication: Not a Cure

So many physical, psychological, and behavioral factors are known to be causes of insomnia that it seems logical that no single medication, or class of medication, could be beneficial for all patients. Indeed, this is the case. Further, sleeping medications of any type provide only symptomatic relief. This means that, although sleep may be improved, the drugs have no direct effect on the cause of the insomnia. *There is no pharmacological cure for insomnia.* Because of this, it is now recognized that treatment of persistent insomnia must focus on the underlying cause(s) of the condition rather than simply producing sleep pharmacologically. This does not mean that medication should never be used in an adjunctive fashion for chronic insomnia. That is, while the underlying causes of disrupted sleep are being addressed directly, relief might be provided *temporarily* for the patient in the form of a sleeping medication. Additionally, as noted above, medications can be useful in some cases of transient or short-term insomnia.

Transient and Short-Term Insomnia

Transient insomnia refers to sleep disruption for as little as a single night or as long as a week. Most people have experienced transient insomnia at some point in their lives—when starting a new job, perhaps, taking college entrance examinations, or facing any momentous or non-routine event. Even the common cold can disturb sleep for a few days. On most nights, sleep is not a problem for these individuals, but when exciting or worrisome situations occur, sleep may be affected until the situation is resolved.

Transient insomnia may also occur if you attempt to sleep "out of synch" with the 24-hour sleepiness/alertness rhythm (see Chapter 11 for a discussion of circadian rhythms). Part of the jet lag syndrome involves poor sleep because rapid travel across time zones results in an inability of the sleep/wake rhythm to adjust rapidly to new environmental times. Therefore, the brain may be in an alert phase when local time indicates it's time to sleep. The result is light, fragmented, and often shortened sleep.

Similarly, the shift worker is required to sleep during a relatively alert portion of his or her sleep/wake rhythm when working the night shift (usually 11:00 p.m. to 7:00 a.m.). With night work, daytime sleep is generally shortened significantly.

In most cases, people simply tolerate these occasional nights of poor sleep, especially if they feel that there are usually no major consequences the following day. However, if the sleep disturbance persists for a few days, or if you can anticipate a situation that may produce a poor night of sleep when you need to be at your best the next day, you might seek medical help. A physician can recommend a medication best suited to your transient sleep difficulties.

Short-term insomnia is a sleep disruption that lasts from one week to a few months. Like transient insomnia, it is usually "triggered" by specific events, such as death of a loved one, medical illness, or other stressors. An example of an individual with short-term insomnia is Mrs. R., a middle-aged woman who is very active in community groups. When confronted with a challenge in her group activities, Mrs. R. has a hard time sleeping until she has arrived at a plan of action. On the average, Mrs. R. would have two or three weeks of poor sleep about every six months when a new, interesting challenge confronted her. Mrs. R. could predict when sleep would be a problem and was bothered considerably by poor sleep. During the day she felt irritable and lacked the energy to resolve her newest issue. On occasion, she would fall asleep unintentionally during meetings, which was quite embarrassing. She sought help from her physician during short-term insomnia episodes. Use of sleeping pills allowed her to tolerate the stress of her group activity much better by preventing sleep loss. Of course, if short-term insomnia is rooted in external causes, it's a good idea to work on those issues directly—even if you can rest with medication. Making behavioral changes may be a way to prevent your short-term insomnia from recurring regularly or developing into a chronic problem. In 1983, the National

Institute of Mental Health sponsored a conference, attended by many experts, for the purpose of developing guidelines for the use of sleep medications. The outcome of this meeting, and the current position of most experts in the area, is that sleeping pills can be very helpful for the treatment of transient and short-term insomnia, particularly for those individuals who are impaired or distressed during the day as a result of poor sleep. The key to determining if a sleep problem is transient or short-term is a history of normal sleep before the causal situation occurs and after it is removed. If you can predict periods of poor sleep, and feel that you are affected significantly the next day, you may wish to discuss intermittent use of sleeping pills with your physician.

Benzodiazepines have been shown by sleep researchers to clearly improve sleep in situations producing transient and short-term insomnia. Since the goal of treatment is to improve sleep *and* daytime functioning, a low dose of a short-acting medication should be used. Remember, though, that there is a risk of discontinuation effects if the dose is too high. A physician should monitor both your drug treatment and drug termination to minimize these effects.

Before considering sleep medication, make sure that you follow the sleep hygiene advice in Chapter 3. Some of your habits or behaviors that generally do not result in sleep problems may contribute to the problem in times of stress. For example, a cup or two of coffee after dinner may not typically disturb your sleep enough for you to perceive it, but when you are also anxious or worried about something, the combination of caffeine and anxiety may produce considerable sleep difficulty. Eliminate those behaviors that may be contributing to

transient insomnia before considering a pharmacological treatment.

Persistent (Chronic) Insomnia

Sleep medication alone is rarely, if ever, the solution
for insomnia that lasts a few months or longer. Persistent insomnia is the result of a cause or causes that will
not spontaneously resolve, often chronic medical or
psychological disorders. In some case, the insomnia is
due to a primary sleep disorder (e.g., sleep apnea).
Although in many cases sleep can be improved temporarily with a sleeping pill, the underlying cause of
the insomnia remains. When the medication is discontinued, the sleep disruption returns. For this reason,
treatment of chronic insomnia must first focus on the
cause of the sleep problem. A specific treatment program
(behavioral, psychological, or medical) must be direct-
ed at that cause for long-term benefit. For example, a
patient who has a problem falling asleep and staying
asleep that is related to arthritic pain would undergo
appropriate treatment for arthritis, such as anti-inflam-
matory or analgesic medications, or physical therapy.
A patient who experiences early morning awakenings
secondary to depression would be treated for depression with anti-depressant medication and/or psychotherapy. Usually, sleep will improve as the distressing
factor is eased.

In some cases, poor sleep will continue despite treatment of the underlying condition. A physician may
then choose to provide relief with sleep medication
even for chronic insomnia problems. In such cases, it is
usually advisable for sleep medication to be given only
for a week or two, or if a longer period is needed, for a

few days per week, rather than every night. Careful attention to sleep hygiene, and an exploration of behavioral treatment options, may avert the need for pharmacological treatment.

General Precautions

Before prescribing a sleeping medication, your physician will want to know specific details about your medical history and medication use. There are several types of patients who should not take sedative-hypnotic medication. These include patients with a history of loud snoring or breathing disorders that might be worsened with ingestion of a sedative, women who are pregnant or breast-feeding, individuals with a history of drug abuse, those taking certain medications that may interact with a sedative, and those whose occupational demands require them to be capable of functioning well upon awakening in the middle of their sleep period (e.g., firemen, physicians, caregivers).

If you take sleeping medication, keep in mind that carry-over sedation may be present the following day. Avoid driving or operating dangerous machinery if you do not feel alert. Realize, too, that one or two nights of disturbed sleep may be experienced following discontinuation of medication, and that this is not sufficient reason to resume taking medication. Never increase your dosage of medication without the approval of your physician. In addition, do not drink alcohol if you are taking sedative-hypnotics: the interaction of the two sedatives reduces the safety margin. Remember that drug therapy is only a temporary treatment, or a supplement to a more comprehensive treatment, and never a cure for sleep difficulty.

6

Relaxation for Sleep

If you suffer from either transient or persistent insomnia, you need to learn and practice relaxation exercises. There are two simple and compelling reasons to do so. First, the experience of insomnia is itself a stress factor. It reduces your ability to function, to cope, and to feel good—both mentally and physically. If you can't function, you feel useless. If you can't cope, then stressors begin to pile up. Second, you tense your muscles in response to these negative feelings and behaviors. You grit your teeth in anticipation of sleeplessness. This increases your body's overall tension level, which only makes your nightly battle worse.

The first step towards healthy sleep is to realize that physical tension and mental anxiety can make coping more difficult. It's a vicious circle—but you can break it by learning to manage the tension in your life. You can learn to identify stress in your body and control its interplay with your sleeplessness.

This chapter presents an array of relaxation exercises, adapted here to suit the special need of insomniacs. The exercises you see in this chapter can be used in preparation for bedtime, during sleep onset, and throughout the course of the night should you happen to awaken. The first three exercises, Deep Breathing, Progressive Muscle Relaxation (PMR), and Autogenic Training (AT), form the basis of any relaxation endeavor. Following these sections, you will find descriptions of ways to use meditation and biofeedback-assisted relaxation. All of these exercises can be done separately or in combination with each other. If you are unfamiliar with using relaxation techniques to reduce tension and anxiety, begin by trying each exercise separately. Give yourself at least one week of daily practice of each, preferably twice a day, before you begin mixing and matching the techniques. After you become comfortable with the feel of each exercise, you can begin to experiment with shortening or lengthening each exercise to suit your needs.

Be sure to practice your technique selection at least once during the day. You will find that with systematic practice, these exercises can be especially effective in counteracting the buildup of anxiety throughout the day. That's a big step towards eliminating a primary cause of insomnia.

Deep Breathing

It's easy to forget about the soothing qualities of fresh air in your lungs. If you've been tense all day following a hectic schedule, and your first chance to relax is in the evening hour just before bed, it's no wonder that relaxing sufficiently to fall asleep is a problem. Deep breathing—also known as "diaphragmatic breathing" or "abdominal breathing"—is one of the most practical ways to relax quickly and effectively. In addition, it helps to counteract oxygen-starved and stressed out bodies by expanding the bottom half of the lung. As you inhale, gently pushing your stomach muscles out, up, and away from your body, you are forcing air into the lower halves of your lungs. Typical breathing is usually rapid and shallow, causing only a partial exchange of oxygen with carbon dioxide. When an insufficient amount of fresh air reaches your lungs, your blood is not cleansed of the waste-carrying carbon dioxide circulated by the blood in preparation of being expelled. Poorly oxygenated blood contributes to undernourished tissue and organs, depression, anxiety, and fatigue. When practiced regularly, deep breathing counteracts these effects and sets off a chain reaction of physical and emotional well-being.

Deep breathing can be practiced anywhere—in the office, riding the bus, driving, at home, before bedtime—while sitting, standing, or lying down. But to become comfortable with the technique, it is recommended that you first focus your attention on abdominal breathing while lying on your back. After abdominal breathing has become automatic for you, it will take only seconds to use it anywhere, anytime, to help relieve tension.

You'll soon find that deep breathing combines nicely with the other forms of relaxation found in this chapter. Before you flip the pages to those, however, focus your attention on deep breathing. It is the foundation on which relaxed bodies are built.

Deep Breathing on Your Back

Lying on your back, place one hand on your chest, and the other on your abdomen. Uncross your legs, allowing them to be spread comfortably apart or bent at the knees with feet flat on floor.

a. Inhale slowly through your nostrils.

b. Feel the breath move through your chest, raising that hand slightly. As the breath reaches your stomach, push your abdomen upwards toward the ceiling, while completing your inhalation. Allow the hand on your abdomen to rise slightly higher than the hand on your chest.

c. Hold for a second, then reverse the process, allowing the breath to pass back out through chest and nostrils. As you exhale, feel your muscles let go of tension. Allow your jaw to unclench as you exhale.

d. Focus on this breathing process twice each day, for a period of 10 to 20 minutes each time. Your body will tell you when you are comfortable with this breathing, and you will soon be able to apply it automatically when your body tenses up.

Deep Breathing on Your Stomach

This is an excellent exercise for practicing abdominal breathing, especially if you have difficulty feeling the movement of the diaphragm while breathing in a sitting or lying position.

a. Lie on your stomach, placing your legs a comfortable distance apart with toes pointed outward. Fold arms in front of your body, resting hands on biceps. Position arms so that the chest does not touch the floor.

b. As you inhale, feel the diaphragmatic motion while in this position.

Points to remember about deep breathing:

1.   Deep breathing can serve as a preventative tool to help you guard against the buildup of tension levels. Monitor yourself throughout the day. At the first signs of stress, take a few moments to do five or six good, deep breaths. You can do this anywhere, anytime, sitting or standing. Simply close your eyes and focus on your breathing, slowing it and deepening it. Do this as many times during the day as necessary to help calm yourself. With persistence, you'll begin to notice the accumulation of calm by the end of the day, rather than the buildup of stress.

2.   Develop the ability to "concentrate passively" on your deep breathing. The concept of passive concentration or passive volition is well known in Eastern philosophy, but less understood in Western culture where striving for perfection is emphasized. Passive concentration enables you to focus on what you are doing, but in such a way that you are comfortably observing your actions, almost as if you were watching yourself from afar. In other words, you allow yourself to breathe deeply rather than forcing yourself to do it perfectly. A common problem with ambitious achievers who are attempting to relax is that they expect themselves to relax perfectly when they command it. They then get frustrated when stray thoughts of business or pleasure interrupt their task. They try to force the thoughts away. They work too hard! If you feel you have to do the deep breathing and other exercises in this chapter "just right" in order for you to be successful, then consider that   you are working against yourself and your goal here—relaxation. Repeat to yourself over and over, "I am ALLOWING myself to relax." See your

extraneous thoughts pass through your mind. Eventually they will cease to clutter your mind, but let that time naturally evolve by itself. Permit yourself *not* to do it just right all the time.

On the Spot Deep Breathing

Whenever you feel troubling thoughts creep into your consciousness, either in the hours before bed or as your head hits the pillow, you probably feel your muscles tensing. Common areas for tension are the abdomen, shoulders, and jaw. *As soon as you feel your muscles tensing,* repeat these simple deep breathing steps:

1. Inhale slowly, pushing the stomach muscles *out.* If it helps, put your hand on your stomach to feel the muscles extending outward as you inhale. This helps elongate your lower lung area, which in turn gets you more breath for the effort, and fills your lungs with healing, soothing oxygen.
2. Exhale slowly, feeling your stomach muscles collapse, and the rest of your muscles melt into the bed.
3. As you exhale, repeat a generic calming phrase to yourself, such as:
   "I am calm"
   "One"
   "Peace"

Or you might prefer a calming phrase specific to sleep inducement, such as:
   "Sleep is coming on"
   "I can sleep now"
   "Sleep is replacing my worries"

Breath Counting Meditation

"Breath counting" is a popular combination of deep breathing and meditation. Instead of using mantras, which seem strange to some people, breath counting simply involves numbering each breath. In this way, you narrow the focus of your attention on the process of relaxation and away from daily distractions.

1. Go to your quiet place and center yourself. Get settled, scan your body for tension, and relax. To help focus your attention, you may choose to close your eyes or gaze at a spot in the room or on the wall.
2. Begin deep breathing. As you exhale, say silently to yourself, "one." Continue to breathe in and out, saying "one" each time you exhale.
3. When thoughts distract you from your breathing, allow yourself to let go of them and return to saying "one." Practice breath counting for at least 10 to 20 minutes at a time.
4. A variation on breath counting is to continue counting each exhalation from one to four: Inhale ... exhale saying "one." Inhale ... exhale saying "two." And so forth. When you reach "four," start over again.

For more about meditation techniques, please see the meditation section in this chapter.

Progressive Muscle Relaxation

Tense people, especially when preoccupied with whether they will go to sleep or not, often have tense muscles. If you find yourself lying in bed and obsessing about a particularly tense muscle, then you may find it harder and harder to relax. Have you ever felt a leg muscle cramp up when you thought about it, even though you tried hard not to? The harder you tried, the more tense you became.

Progressive Muscle Relaxation (PMR) was developed 40 years ago by a doctor named Edmund Jacobson. He wanted his patients to be able to differentiate clearly between a tensed and a relaxed muscle, and so he developed a process that intentionally contracted and released the tensed muscle. To do PMR, all you have to do is focus on the cramped muscle, tense it gently, and then relax it. You can relax your whole body this way. You begin with a muscle group at one end of your body, for example your toes or facial muscles, and systematically work up or down through as many muscle groups as you choose.

This exercise can be a very effective way to learn about the AMOUNT of muscle tension you carry in your body. It will also help you feel the sharp contrast between tensed muscles and relaxed muscles. It is easy to walk around with clenched teeth or fists all day, and not even realize it. Until, that is, the end of the day when you have a tension headache or a sore shoulder. Sometimes when you think you have relaxed your muscles, they may still be contracted tightly, causing muscle fatigue, poor circulation, cramping, and stiffness. Ease into this exercise slowly and don't strain yourself.

You will be focusing on four major groups of muscles in the body:

1. Hands, forearms, and biceps
2. Thighs, buttocks, calves, and feet
3. Chest, stomach, and lower back

4. Head, face, throat, neck, and shoulders. Facial muscles include forehead, cheeks, nose, eyes, jaws, lips, and tongue.

Once you have read through the description below, try to spend at least 20 minutes per day on each muscle group. It is usually helpful to follow along with a tape at first. You can buy a pre-made tape at many bookstores or sleep labs, or make one yourself using the script below.

Begin Progressive Muscle Relaxation by lying down or sitting in a comfortable chair with your head supported. Take several deep breaths, releasing each breath slowly. This deep and natural breathing is your cue to begin your relaxation session.

a. Focus on the first group of muscles—your right hand, arm, and bicep. Make a fist, clenching as hard as you can. Hold that tension, feeling it creep up your arm towards your shoulder. Hold it until you begin to feel a gentle cramping or burning sensation. You may notice your muscles quiver slightly.

b. Now relax, feeling the muscles go limp. Feel the warming blood flow through your arm into your hand and fingers. Notice the contrast between what it felt like when it was tense, and what it feels like now when it is relaxed.

c. Repeat this twice more. Remember to pay attention to your breathing as you tense and relax. Does your breathing begin to get shallow? Make sure you are not unconsciously holding your breath.

d. Now notice how the right arm and hand feel compared to the left arm and hand. Move to your left hand, arm, and bicep to repeat the exercise three times.

After a few days of this muscle group, move on to the second group, thighs, buttocks, calves, and feet. Repeat the same procedure as above, alternating sides of your body.

a. Focus on your right foot and calf. Tighten them as hard as you can. You can either pull your foot upward, or stretch your foot outward by pointing your toe. Hold the tension, feeling it creep up your leg toward your torso. Hold the tension till you begin to feel a slight cramping, burning sensation.

b. Now relax, feeling the muscles go limp. Feel the warming blood flow through your calf and foot. Notice the contrast between what your muscles felt like when you were tense, and what they feel like now that you are relaxed.

c. Repeat this procedure twice more. Remember to pay attention to your breathing as you tense and relax. Does your breathing begin to get shallow? Make sure you are not unconsciously holding your breath.

d. Now notice how the right calf and foot feel in comparison to the left calf and foot. Focus on your left calf and foot and repeat the exercise three times.

e. Now focus on your right leg again. Tense your thigh and buttocks as you tense your foot and calf. Tense as hard as you can, until you begin to feel a slight cramping and burning sensation.

f. Now relax, feeling all the muscles in your right leg go limp. Feel the warming blood flow through your buttocks, thigh, calf, and foot. Notice the contrast between what your leg felt like when it was tense, and what it feels like now when it is relaxed.

g. Repeat this procedure twice more. Remember to do relaxed and natural breathing. Notice how your right leg feels in comparison to your left leg.

h. Move to you left leg, adding the buttocks and thigh to your left foot and calf. Repeat the exercise three times.

Spend the next two to three days of your practice on group 3: chest, stomach, and lower back. Remember to breathe deeply and exhale slowly as you release the tension in your stomach. If you have low back pain, proceed cautiously with the tensing of your back muscles. Contract the muscles as much as you can, but do not strain or overdo it.

a. Focus on your chest, stomach, and lower back. Tense those areas, lightly pushing your lower back into the bed or chair as you contract your abdominal muscles and shrug your shoulders. Hold the tension until you begin to feel a slightly cramping, burning sensation.

b. Now relax, feeling the muscles go limp. Feel the warming blood flow through your lower back, stomach, and chest. Notice the contrast between what it felt like when these areas were tense, and what it feels like now when they are relaxed.

c. Repeat this procedure twice more. Remember to do relaxed and natural breathing.

Now move on to the next muscle group: the head, face, neck, and shoulder muscles. Pay special attention to the facial muscles. They are extremely sensitive to stress and anxiety. Your jaw muscles are so powerful that you can be tensing them all day without realizing it. You can use the following script:

Facial PMR

Turning attention to your head, wrinkle your forehead as tight as you can. Lift your eyebrows as high as they will go ... Now relax and smooth it out. Let yourself imagine your entire forehead and scalp becoming smooth and at rest. Repeat....

Now frown and notice the strain spreading throughout your forehead. Where else is it tense? Your jaw? Your neck? Let go. Allow your brow to become smooth again. Close your eyes, now squint them tighter. Scan for tension. Relax your eyes. Let them remain closed gently and comfortably.

Now clench your jaw. Bite hard. Notice the tension throughout your jaw. This muscle is very powerful, and you may not be aware of the amount of tension it can hold. Relax your jaw. When the jaw is relaxed, your lips will be slightly parted. Let yourself really appreciate the contrast between tension and relaxation. Think of your jaw as two unconnected halves—top and bottom untouching.

Now press your tongue against the roof of your mouth. Push it hard against the top. Feel the ache in the back of your mouth and the tip of your tongue. Relax. Press your lips now, purse them into an "O." Relax your lips. Notice that your forehead, scalp, eyes, jaw, tongue, and lips are all relaxed.

A Variation on Progressive Muscle Relaxation: Differential Relaxation

Differential relaxation simply means tensing and relaxing as you would with PMR, but doing it with diagonal muscle groups at the same time. For example, starting with muscle groups 1 and 2, tense your right arm and hand and left leg and foot at the same time. Also release simultaneously. As you tense, pay attention to the sides of your body you are not tensing. (Left arm, hand and right leg, foot). This may take some practice.

The purpose of differential relaxation is to introduce you to a slightly more complex exercise that more closely resembles your daily activity. A common example is that when you drive, you often unconsciously clench your teeth and jaw in response to traffic or the normal wear and tear of driving. This locks in needless additional tension. Of course, you don't want to relax *all* of your body while driving. You need to keep your leg and foot tense and alert on the accelerator pedal. Differential relaxation teaches you how to tense one part of the body, while keeping the other relaxed.

As you practice this exercise, pay attention to the feeling of tension on the tense side *and* the feeling of relaxation on the relaxed side. By doing so simultaneously, you are encouraging your brain to develop a multiple capacity for relaxing. In other words, you are learning to be alert and relaxed at the same time. This exercise will help you to learn to easily adapt other forms of relaxation to your everyday activity.

Remember not to rush through each muscle group while practicing PMR or differential relaxation. Allow yourself the luxury of a sufficient amount of time per muscle group.

You may also find it useful to use the following expressions while releasing your muscle tension:

> "Let go of the tension."
> "Relax and smooth out the muscles."
> "Let the tension dissolve away."
> "Let go more and more."

Autogenic Training

In the 1930s, two physicians named Johannes Schultz and Wolfgang Luthe found that they could help their patients reduce fatigue by teaching them to self-generate feelings of heaviness and warmth in their extremities. Rather than working physically with the muscles as with PMR, Autogenic Training (AT) works on the principle that the brain can give messages of warmth and relaxation to the blood vessels, which in turn relax your muscles and even internal organs.

Sometimes the process of contracting/releasing is more stimulating than relaxing, and you might find that you prefer a more passive exercise. Insomniacs are renowned for their high anxiety levels, and sometimes a passive activity distracts a highly anxious person more effectively that a physical activity. In addition, studies show that AT encourages the actual flow of blood to the extremities. Stressed out people have a tendency towards poorer circulation. Autogenic Training can help to reverse this, allowing the hands and feet to be warmer because of the better blood flow. This helps you feel more overall relaxation. It also demonstrates your brain's tremendous control over your body. After you feel your body responding to the standard Autogenics phrases below, you can customize the phrases to suit your imagination. For example, you might warm your hands and then move them to a sore muscle, as if your hands were a hot-water bottle. Or, move your warmed hands to your forehead. Imagine that the added warmth is melting away all obsessive and distracting thoughts.

You will focus on the same four muscle groups as you did with Progressive Muscle Relaxation.

1. Hands and arms
2. Thighs, buttocks, legs, and feet
3. Chest, stomach, and lower back
4. Head, face, throat, neck, and shoulders

Spend at least 20 minutes per day on each muscle group, and approximately one full week of practice for each group. Usually it is helpful to follow along with a tape at first. You can buy a pre-made tape, or make one yourself using the script below (adapted from the cassette tape series *The Relaxation Training Program* by Thomas Budzinski).

Begin Autogenics by lying down or sitting in a comfortable chair with your head supported. Take several deep breaths, releasing each breath slowly. This deep and natural breathing is your cue to begin your relaxation session.

1. Focus on the first muscle group—your right hand and arm. Lay your arm flat on an armrest, a table top, or your lap. Your aim is to become intensely aware of the muscles and fibers in your arm and hand— and then let them go. Feel the warmth and weight as you repeat the phrases:

   "My right hand is heavy."
   "My right hand is heavy and warm."
   "My right hand is letting go."

   "My right arm is heavy."
   "My right arm is heavy and warm."
   "My right arm is letting go."

Repeat each set of phrases twice, then move to your left hand and arm. Feel your arm float on its own as you allow your blood to flow from your shoulder through your elbow to the tips of your fingers.

"My left hand is heavy."
"My left hand is heavy and warm."
"My left hand is letting go."

"My left arm is heavy."
"My left arm is heavy and warm."
"My left arm is letting go."

2. After several days on the first group, move on to the second group: your feet, calves, thighs, and buttocks. Repeat these phrases to yourself:

"My right leg is heavy."
"My right leg is heavy and warm."
"My right leg is letting go."

"My left leg is heavy."
"My left leg is heavy and warm."
"My left leg is letting go."

"My right thigh is heavy."
"My right thigh is heavy and warm."
"My right thigh is letting go."

"My left thigh is heavy."
"My left thigh is heavy and warm."
"My left thigh is letting go."

"My buttocks are heavy."
"My buttocks are heavy and warm."
"My buttocks are letting go."

3. Next, move to group 3, stomach, chest, and lower back. Focus on each area separately and repeat to yourself these phrases:

"My stomach is heavy."
"My stomach is heavy and warm."
"My stomach is letting go."

"My chest is heavy."
"My chest is heavy and warm."
"My chest is letting go."

"My lower back is heavy."
"My lower back is heavy and warm."
"My lower back is letting go."

4. Next focus on group 4, shoulders, neck, throat, face, and head. Repeat these phrases to yourself, focusing first on your shoulders, then neck and throat, then head and face.

"My shoulders are heavy."
"My shoulders are heavy and warm."
"My shoulders are letting go."

"My neck and throat are heavy."
"My neck and throat are heavy and warm."
"My neck and throat are letting go."

"My head and face are heavy."
"My head and face are heavy and warm."
"My head and face are letting go."

As you become comfortable and adept at Autogenic phrases, you can add additional instructions, such as "My right arm is loose and limp." Remember to check your breathing periodically to make sure you are breathing by imagining the blood flowing to your extremities as you exhale.

It is helpful and natural to incorporate imagery into your Autogenic work. Some examples might be to imagine the sun warming your hands as you repeat the phrases, or that you are lying in a warm bath, or any other scene that comes to mind and represents heaviness and warmth.

These additional expressions may be used while you repeat the Autogenic phrases, or repeat them to yourself at the end of your session (from *The Relaxation and Stress Reduction Workbook*).

"I feel quiet."

"My whole body feel quiet, heavy, comfortable, and relaxed."

"My mind is quiet."

"I withdraw my thoughts from the surroundings and I feel serene and still."

"My thoughts are turned inward and I am at ease."

"Deep within my mind, I can visualize and experience myself as relaxed and comfortable and still."

"I feel an inward quietness."

Remember to adopt an attitude of passive concentration while practicing your Autogenic techniques. This means, do not force yourself to concentrate. Rather, ALLOW yourself to focus on the exercises. When extraneous thoughts intrude upon your concentration, simply allow them to pass through your mind. Eventually, with practice, they will become less numerous and intrusive.

Add Deep Breathing to your repetitions of Autogenic phrases: Make use of the healing properties of oxygen and deep breathing by including deep breathing with your AT phrases. In between each body section that you are relaxing, pay attention to your breathing. Does your stomach continue to stay relaxed as you repeat the AT phrases? If not, breathe deeply. As you exhale, feel your jaw drop open, and the healing warmth of oxygenated blood rush into each muscle.

Meditation

Meditation can be practiced just before bed or while in bed. It is both simple and effective. The idea may at first seem foreign to you, but meditation is actually very similar in process to other relaxation exercises where you minimize distractions and narrow your focus of attention. Specifically, meditation involves repetition of a "mantra," a word or phrase that you find particularly pleasant and comforting. As you repeat this word over and over, you permit distracting thoughts, sounds, and feelings to pass by uncritically. Without judging them or yourself, you allow these negative thoughts and feelings to fade away, enabling you to return to your mantra.

Meditation is similar to self-hypnosis in that once you are in a very relaxed state, your consciousness becomes uncluttered and open to suggestion. At this point you are able to give yourself soothing suggestions embodied by the mantra. With hypnosis, you are able to give yourself direct healing commands.

If you choose to practice meditation at some point during the day in preparation for your bedtime session, remember to pay attention to the following four major components of meditation:

1. Choose a quiet place in which to meditate. Turn down the volume on the answering machine, or turn the phone off altogether. Minimize external distractions wherever possible.
2. Choose a comfortable position that can be maintained for about 20 minutes causing discomfort. Avoid meditating within two hours of a heavy meal, since digestion interferes with your comfort.

3. It is helpful to select an object to dwell upon: a word or sound repetition, an object or symbol to gaze at or imagine, even a specific feeling or thought. As distracting thoughts enter your mind, you can let them pass while returning to the chosen object of focus.

4. Maintain a passive attitude. When distracting thoughts occur, let go of them, but don't force them to leave. Don't judge yourself or your ability to perform the meditative process. Assume an objective, uncritical stance. Imagine yourself observing yourself repeating your mantra effortlessly and comfortably.

A variation of the meditative technique is the breath counting exercise described in the "Deep Breathing" section of this chapter. For more information about self-hypnosis, see Chapter 7.

Relaxation Aided by Biofeedback

Biofeedback involves the use of instruments to measure muscle tension, blood flow, heart rate, and more. These measurements are indicators of your stress level. For example, if you unknowingly clench your jaw, this tends to increase the muscle tension in your face, neck, and shoulders. If you were hooked up to a biofeedback machine, it would record a high level of muscle contractions in that area, indicating a high level of muscle tension there. Muscle tension levels are typically measured with surface electrodes placed on the forehead area. These reveal tension levels in the face, jaw, neck, and shoulders. Biofeedback is not at all painful (or even scary). In fact, it's a very relaxing procedure. You are usually given audio cues (a beeping tone) or visual cues (computer graphs) to tell you how much your muscles are letting go of the tension. As you relax, the graphs diminish and the tone beeps lower and lower.

Sometimes hand temperatures reflect your typical response to stress. Remember the "mood rings" of the 1960s? They operated on this principle. As you become anxious, blood flow is constricted and your extremities can become cold as ice. In biofeedback, electrodes are placed on your fingertips, and you are given information as to when you are becoming warmer, and thus more relaxed.

The biofeedback procedure is intended as a teaching aid. Once you know how it feels to be relaxed and calm according to the instruments, you can transfer that learning to daily activities and nighttime sleep preparation. While most equipment is too cumbersome and expensive to have at home, some simplified versions of biofeedback instruments are available at reasonable prices. These are adequate in reminding you of your tension levels.

Common at-home modified versions of biofeedback equipment are "temperature rings" and "stress dots." As a preventative tool, the ring functions as an early warning system. It has a temperature range of 67 to 94 degrees, with little dots that light up at each point on the range. If you notice your temperature dropping, indicating a possible increase in tension levels, you can use this information as a cue to take note of your situation. Are you feeling anxious? Angry? Or are you simply in a cold room? Once you have this answer, you can apply a therapeutic technique: autogenics and imagery might warm your hands and focus and soothe your mind. One source of information on home biofeedback is available in a brochure from FUTUREHEALTH, Inc., Dept. P-100, P.O. Box 947, Bensalem, Pa 19020.

Stress dots also provide you with a general idea of your temperature range. You peel the dot from a piece of paper and attach it your hand. The dot changes color as your hands change from cool to warm. Stress dots can be ordered from Mindbody, Inc., 50 Maple Pl., Manhasset, NY 11030.

You can incorporate these aids as part of your night-time ritual. If you are choosing to do a combination of Deep Breathing and Meditation as your pre-bed procedure, use the relaxation aids to verify your relaxation response.

Further Reading

The American Medical. Association. *Better Sleep.* New York: Random House, 1984.

Davis, Martha, Matthew McKay; Elizabeth Eshelman. *The Relaxation & Stress Reduction Workbook.* Oakland, CA: New Harbinger Publications, 1982.

Dryer, Bernard, M.D.; Ellen S. Kaplan. *Inside Insomnia. How to Sleep Better Tonight.* New York: Villard Books, 1986.

Lacks, Patricia. *Behavioral Treatment For Persistent Insomnia.* New York: Pergamon Press, 1987.

7

Self-Hypnosis and Imagery

The powerful combination of self-hypnosis and imagery has repeatedly proven to help reprogram poor sleep habits. Self-hypnosis employs the use of simple suggestions in a trance state that are geared to helping you fall asleep and maintain sleep. Imagery—the visualization of anything you find pleasant and sleep inducing—usually springs into your unconscious mind while you are in a trance state, and can be intentionally shaped to reinforce hypnotic suggestions and post-hypnotic cues. These two strategies combine naturally to provide you with an effective array of techniques to help you sleep better. It takes practice to perfect them, but the basics can be learned in under an hour.

Self-Hypnosis Techniques

The word "hypnosis" often invokes images of things mysterious, but the experience commonly occurs in many unspectacular ways throughout the day. You can probably identify several times in the past week when you lost yourself in concentration, perhaps when driving or watching TV. These states are examples of hypnotic trances which can be adapted to focus intentionally on an area of difficulty in your life, such as insomnia.

There is a physical difference between sleep and an hypnotic state. In sleep you are not conscious or aware of the world; in hypnosis you are in a calm, peaceable state, but aware. You use hypnosis to pass through to the unconsciousness of sleep. Your signal for coming out of the trance is when you actually fall asleep. This way you can be assured that you will awaken if you need to. In fact, you are in complete control of your trance state at all times. You can control when to terminate the trance and when to fall peacefully into sleep.

Self-hypnosis uses an induction, or a script, to bring about a trance state. Inductions vary in style and content. Concerning style, you may find that you respond readily to an induction that uses a highly directive, authoritative voice, such as:

"You will listen to my voice. My voice will help you relax as deeply as possible. I want you to begin to relax now. As you relax deeper and deeper you will respond to the suggestions I give you."

Or, you may prefer a softer, more passive voice in your induction, such as:

"As you listen to my voice, allow it to help you relax. You can let my voice help you relax as deeply as possible. As you relax more and more deeply, just imagine yourself in a peaceful place. It may be by the ocean or in the mountains. Any place is fine. Imagine how wonderful you feel in this place. Imagine how peaceful you feel there. Now let yourself relax even more deeply, and as you relax, allow yourself to embrace the suggestion that I am about to give you."

You can choose to induce a trance by selecting any of the relaxation exercises described in this book. A popular combination is deep breathing and systematic muscle relaxation. Some people prefer to use the "fixation" method of hypnotic induction, where attention is drawn to a very narrow point. For example, you can stare into a flickering candle to practice this type of induction. A typical induction might sound like this:

"Watch the flame burn and flicker and keep your eyes on the flame and concentrate on it. Watch the flame flicker and keep your eyes on the flame. As you watch the flame burning, your eyes will become heavy, become heavy, and your eyes will grow heavier and heavier … and heavier … heavier … until they close."

You might want to experiment with the different induction approaches and custom design one to suit your needs. Effective inductions may be quite different from one another, but they must all bring about these results:

- Relaxation of body and mind
- Narrowed focus of attention
- Reduced awareness of external environment and everyday concerns
- Greater internal awareness of sensations
- A trance state

All hypnosis is essentially self-hypnosis. When hypnosis is practiced in a clinic or hospital, a trained therapist guides you through the steps, which you still enact on your own. Sometimes it is useful to begin hypnosis practice under the guidance of a trained clinician. He or she can introduce you to the techniques, guide you in their appropriate uses, and motivate you to follow through on your home practice. Of course, if you already have the motivation, you can use this book as your guide and proceed on your own.

As with the rest of the self-help strategies outlined in this book, self-hypnosis cannot serve as the sole treatment if you suspect you have an underlying medical condition.

Hypnotic Inductions

The following is a general induction adapted for insomniacs. The induction begins with suggestions for overall relaxation, and ends with specific post-hypnotic sleep instructions. Feel free to insert phrases that customize the induction to suit your particular needs. You can choose to read over an induction to familiarize yourself with it, and then repeat it from memory as you relax. Or you may find it easier to make a tape recording of yourself or a friend reading the induction. If you choose to record an induction, here are some suggestions for recording the sample induction that follows.

1. Read the induction aloud several times in order to become familiar and comfortable with its content. When recording, speak slowly and in a monotone, keeping your voice level and your words evenly spaced. You will need to experiment with tone and stress until you are satisfied with the way the induction sounds.

2. Choose a location for recording free of any sounds that may be picked up on the tape, such as clocks, television, telephone, or doorbell. You will also need to alert your family or roommates. Make sure they understand that they are not to inter-

rupt you or make any other sounds that can be heard on tape.
3. Put on comfortable clothing and get into a comfortable position. You may want to lie down, sit in a rocking chair, or sit at your desk with your feet up. Whatever your preferred position, make sure it is one that will be comfortable throughout the entire recording session. If you are shifting around or feeling physically uncomfortable, this discomfort will be reflected in the tone and quality of your voice.

Six Sleep Induction Steps

Step 1. Beginning the induction. The induction begins by focusing your attention on your breathing and inner sensations. As you focus inward, your awareness of external surroundings will decrease. By breathing deeply, you become aware of your internal sensations. You introduce your body to relaxation. Your pulse slows, your breathing slows, you begin to withdraw, and you can direct your attention to the suggestions that are given to you.

Step 2. Systematic relaxation of the body. As the induction directs you to concentrate on relaxing every muscle in your body, your mind will also become more relaxed. You will experience an increased awareness of internal functions and an increased receptivity of the senses.

Step 3. Creating imagery of deeper relaxation. The induction's image of drifting down deeper and deeper helps you to enter a deeper trance. Tension in your shoulders is released by an image of weight being lifted from your shoulders. Any difference in your bodily sensations will support the suggestion that a change is taking place. It does not matter whether the direction specified in the induction is upward or downward, so long as the image of rising or descending make it possible for you to experience a change in your physical feelings.

Step 4. Deepening the trance. To help you deepen your trance or "go down," you count backwards from ten to one. In order to return to full consciousness or "come up," you count forward from one to ten. The induction uses the image of a staircase with 10 steps, but you can substitute any image you like in order to enhance the feeling of going down. The image of an elevator descending 10 floors is a popular alternative.

At this stage your limbs become limp or stiff. Your attention will have narrowed, and suggestibility will heighten. The surrounding environment will be closed out.

Step 5. The special place. The special place you choose to imagine will be one that is unique to you and your experience. It can be a place you have actually visited or one that you imagine. The place does not have to be real, or even possible. You can be sitting on a big blue pillow floating on the surface of a quiet sea. You can be stretched out in a hammock suspended in space. You can be in a cave of clouds. Your special place must be one in which you can be alone and it must produce a positive feeling in you. It is in this special place that you will have an increased receptivity to further suggestions. That is, once a peaceful feeling is established, you will be responsive to imagery that reinforces and supports post-hypnotic suggestions. Make sure, as you visualize your special place, that you try to include sights, sounds, and physical sensations (temperature, texture) in the image.

Step 6. Suggesting sleep. Now you begin to put away your worries and negative thoughts. You suggest that you are drifting into a sound and restful sleep. You may also add here your own customized suggestion to encourage a deep, refreshing sleep.

Customize Your Induction for Sleep

The following is a list of specific sleep instructions that can be inserted into the induction. Or, you can write your own.

- I will stay asleep all night.
- I won't wake up until it's time.
- I will waken refreshed and alert.
- Falling asleep is my signal that I am out of a trance and going into deep sleep.
- I will get up in the night to use the bathroom if needed, but I will fall asleep again easily.
- All thoughts of daytime anxieties are unnecessary; I am allowing them to pass through my conscious awareness and disappear.
- I will dream as usual. (Hypnosis will not affect my dreams.)
- I will gradually become more and more drowsy. In just a few minutes I will be able to fall asleep, and sleep peacefully all night.
- I can turn off anger and guilt because I am the one who turns it *on.* I will relax my body and breathe deeply.

Write your own: _____

_____

Hypnotic Induction for Insomnia

Take a nice deep breath, close your eyes, and begin to relax. Just think about relaxing every muscle in your body from the top of your head to the tips of your toes. Just begin to relax. And begin to notice how very comfortable your body is beginning to feel. You are supported, so you can just let go and relax. Inhale and exhale. Notice your breathing; notice the rhythm of your breathing and relax your breathing for a moment.

Be aware of normal sounds around you. These sounds are unimportant, discard them, whatever you hear from now on will only help to relax you. And as you exhale, release any tension, any stress from any part of your body, mind, and thought; just let that stress go. Just feel any stressful thoughts rushing through your mind, feel them begin to wind down, wind down, wind down, and relax.

And begin with letting all the muscles in your face relax, especially your jaw; let your teeth part just a little bit and relax this area.This is a place where tension and stress gather, so be sure to relax your jaw and feel that relaxation go into your temples. Relax the muscles in your temples and as you think about relaxing these muscles they will relax. Feel them relax and as you relax you'll be able to just drift and float into a deeper and deeper level of total relaxation. You will continue to relax and now let all of the muscles in your forehead relax. Feel those muscle smooth, smooth and relax, and rest your eyes. Just imagine your eyelids feeling so comfortable, so heavy, so heavy, so relaxed.

And now let all of the muscles in the back of your neck and shoulders relax, feel a heavy, heavy weight being lifted off your shoulders, and you feel relieved, lighter and more relaxed. And all of the muscles in the back of your neck and shoulders relax, and feel that soothing relaxation go down your back, down, down, down, to the lower part of your back, and those muscles let go and with every breath you inhale just feel your body drifting, floating, down deeper, down deeper, down deeper into total relaxation.

Let your muscles go, relaxing more and more. Let all the muscles in your shoulders, running down your arms to your fingertips, relax. And let your arms feel so heavy, so heavy, so heavy, so comfortable, so relaxed. You may have tingling in your fingertips. That's perfectly fine. You may have warmth in the palms of your hands, and that's fine. And you may feel that you can barely lift your arms, they are so relaxed, they are so heavy, so heavy, so relaxed. And now you inhale once again and relax your chest muscles. And now as you exhale, feel your stomach muscles relax. As you exhale, relax all the muscles in your stomach, let them go, and all the muscles in your legs, feel them relax, and all of the muscles in your legs, so completely relaxed right to the tips of your toes.

Notice how very comfortable your body feels, just drifting and floating, deeper, deeper, deeper relaxed. And as you are relaxing deeper and deeper, imagine a beautiful staircase. There are ten steps, and the steps lead you to a special and peaceful and beautiful place. In a moment you can begin to imagine taking a safe and gentle and easy step down, down, down on the staircase, leading you to a very peaceful, a very special place for you. You can imagine it to be any place you choose, perhaps you would enjoy a beach or ocean with clean, fresh air, or the mountains with a stream; any place is perfectly fine.

In a moment I'm going to count backwards from ten to one and you can imagine taking the steps down and as you take each step, feel your body relax, more and more feel it just drift down, down each step, and relax even deeper, ten, relax even deeper, nine ... eight ... seven ... six ... five ... four ...

three ... two ... one ... deeper, deeper, deeper, relaxed. And now imagine a peaceful and special place. You can imagine this special place and perhaps you can even feel it. You are in a [INSERT SPECIAL PLACE]. You are alone and there is no one to disturb you. This is the most peaceful place in the world for you. Imagine yourself there and feel that sense of peace flow through you and sense of well-being and enjoy these positive feelings and keep them with you. Allow these positive feelings to grow stronger and stronger, feeling at peace with a sense of well-being. And now just linger in your special place. There is no place to go, nothing to do. Just rest and let yourself drift and float, drift and float into a sound and restful sleep. Just let yourself drift deeper and deeper into sleep.

And now become aware of how comfortable you feel, so relaxed, your head and shoulders are in just the right position, your back is supported and you are becoming less and less aware of all the normal sounds of your surroundings, and as you drift deeper and deeper you may experience a negative thought or worry trying to surface in your mind, trying to disrupt your slumber, trying to disrupt your rest. Simply take that thought, sweep it up as you would sweep up crumbs from the floor and place that thought or worry into a box. The box has a nice tight lid. Put the lid on the box and place the box on the top shelf of your closet. You can go back to that box at another time, a time that is more appropriate, a time that will not interfere with your sleep. So as these unwanted thoughts appear, sweep them up and place them in the box, put a lid on the box and place it on the top shelf of your closet and let them go. Let them go and continue to drift deeper and deeper into sleep.

Shift your thoughts back to your positive thoughts and positive statements. Just let these thoughts flow through your mind, thoughts such as "I am a worthwhile person."

[PAUSE] "I have accomplished many good things." [PAUSE] "I have reached positive goals." [PAUSE] Just let your own positive ideas flow through your mind. Let them flow and drift, becoming stronger and stronger as you drift, becoming stronger and stronger as you drift deeper and deeper into sleep. You may begin to see them slowly fade, slowly fade as you become even more relaxed, more sleepy, more drowsy, more relaxed. Just imagine yourself in your peaceful and special place, smiling, feeling so good, so comfortable, so relaxed. [PAUSE] And from your special place you can easily drift into a sound and restful sleep, a sound and restful sleep, undisturbed in a sound and restful sleep. You sleep throughout the night in a sound and restful sleep.

If you should awaken you simply imagine your special place once again, and drift easily back into a sound and restful sleep, a sound and restful sleep. Your breathing becomes so relaxed, your thoughts wind down, wind down, wind down, and relax. You drift and float into a sound and restful sleep, undisturbed throughout the night. You will awaken at your designated time feeling rested and refreshed.

Now there's nothing to do, nothing to think about, nothing to do but enjoy your special place, your special place that is so peaceful for you, so relaxing. Just imagine how it feels to relax in your special place. You may become aware of how clean and fresh your special place smells, or you may become aware of the different sounds of your special place, such as birds singing in the background, or water cascading over rocks in a stream. Or you may become aware of how warm the sun feels as you lounge in a hammock, or how cool the breeze feels from the ocean air. Or you may experience something else that is unique and wonderful in your special place. Just experience it, drift and float, all thoughts just fading, drifting into a sound and restful sleep. Just drift into a comfortable, cozy, restful sleep, your body feeling heavy *and relaxed as you sink into your bed, so relaxed, just drifting into sleep [PAUSE], sleep [PAUSE], sleep [PAUSE, SOFTLY REPEAT SLEEP THREE MORE TIMES], sleep ... sleep ... sleep ...*

More Post-Hypnotic Suggestions

A cornerstone of the self-hypnotic technique is to introduce post-hypnotic suggestions into your trance statements. These suggestions, which are given during the induction and carried out at some other time in the day, serve as cues to reinforce your sleep goals. For example, you may give yourself the suggestion that whenever you see a clock, you are reminded of your growing sense of mastery and control over your insomnia. Post-hypnotic cues are most effective if they're incorporated into your daily pre-bed rituals. Dr. Brian Alman, in his book *Self-Hypnosis: A Complete Manual for Health and Self-Change*, suggests that you give yourself these post-hypnotic suggestions while in a trance:

"I may notice that when I brush my teeth in the evening, just before bed, as I clean my teeth I can also clean my mind of worry, tension, and anxiety."

"As I take off my robe and hang it on the hook, I may also imagine that on my robe are pinned all of my problems, troubles, and worries from the day. I can see them now, like index cards or signs upon which are written all the worries that might keep me from sleeping. They're too small to read, but I feel that as I lift off my robe the weight of these worries and anxieties are lifted off me also. The robe and these worries are in the

---

Adapted from *Hypnosis for Change*, Second Edition, by Josie Hadley and Carol Staudacher. New Harbinger Publications, 1989.

closet, and I can put them on tomorrow if I wish. But tonight I can sleep without them."

Self-Hypnosis for Napping

For those of you with chronic insomnia, it is best if you avoid napping altogether. However, a low point in the body's natural rhythms generally occurs between 2:00 and 5:00 p.m., encouraging that napping feeling each day. Some people, if they have the luxury, are greatly refreshed by a respite from the day's events at this time. Others feel that they are unable to relax enough to take a nap. If you know that you would feel refreshed by a nap, but worry that it might last too long or disrupt your nighttime sleep, you can use hypnosis as a tool to facilitate and regulate these breaks. The relaxed hypnotic state can even serve as a satisfying replacement for napping.

The idea is to suggest to yourself that you will keep your nap brief (10 to 20 minutes). You won't actually fall into sleep, but will use the induction techniques just before sleep to relax yourself. You'll find that using self-hypnosis in this way can be invigorating, whereas falling into a deep sleep can leave you groggy and fatigued for the rest of the day.

If you are a student studying for exams and feel forced to sleep in shifts, you can try using these self-hypnotic breaks to energize yourself and supplement your sleep. Or, if you're a shift worker and find that you have to grab sleep when you can, you may want to try to adapt one of these inductions to help you relax more quickly and efficiently. Choose one of the inductions in this chapter to enter the trance, and insert the following suggestion while in the trance:

"Now that I am relaxed and comfortable, I know that I can slip easily into sleep. However, I choose instead to remain in this refreshing state, peaceful and aware. As I gradually leave this state and reenter wakefulness, I will fill refreshed, alert, and ready for the rest of the day.

"I can return to a refreshed and alert state by counting from one to five. As I get closer to five my eyes will open … I will feel more refreshed and more alert. One … two … three … four … five … I am awake, alert, and feeling good."

A Word of Caution

Self-hypnosis may not be effective or advisable for those of you who are not sleeping because of emotional trauma, illness, or injury. Please consult a medical professional if you have a physical illness or injury, or a mental health professional if you are suffering from emotional trauma, before embarking on a self-hypnosis program. Dr. Charles Holland, a psychologist in Roanoke, Virginia, regularly teaches hypnosis for sleep and other psychological disorders. He suggests that if you are going through a crisis period, do *not* lie in bed or sit in a dark, dimly lit room and attempt to force yourself into hypnosis. This only fosters obsessive thinking, which heightens anxiety. Obsessing leads to feelings of failure and disappointment in yourself. Obsessing also heightens fearfulness. Fearfulness obstructs the relaxed pathways to sleep.

Instead, Dr. Holland suggests that you "get vertical and get light." This means that you get out of bed, turn on some lights, and do some relatively simple activity such as reading. This helps you avoid working yourself into a frenzy. You could also seek out a professional counselor, therapist, or minister. If consulting these persons is not an option, give yourself permission to work through your anxiety gradually. Tell your pet about it. Write about it.

Please refer to Chapters 8 and 9 on managing your obsessions and conditioning insomnia techniques for more information about ways to save yourself from obsessing about sleep and other problems.

Imagery

Imagery is a natural part of self-hypnosis. Mental pictures you create spontaneously or deliberately will enhance your trance state. These pictures can be literal, such as picturing an escalator going down to help you relax and deepen your trance. Or these pictures can be symbolic of overall pleasant feelings, such as the feeling you get when you see, hear, and smell ocean waves crashing upon the beach.

Once you appreciate the power of visualizing images, you are free to experiment with as many images as possible. Just make sure that they are positive, pleasurable images that make you feel good. If negative, self-defeating images pop into your mind, don't berate yourself, squeezing your eyes tight and trying to force them out of your head. Instead, use the following imagery to "allow" them to pass out of your consciousness.

> See the negative words or images go floating past you one by one, each one on a log bobbing slowly on a stream. The stream flows away from you and the logs bob out of sight.
> See each negative word or image pasted on a balloon. Feel a gentle breeze on your face. See the

balloons blow back and forth in the air, finally being carried up and off into the sky.

If you try to force unpleasant thoughts away and they insist on returning, you may find yourself getting more frustrated and aroused by the minute. This only makes it harder for you to relax. Simply repeat the above techniques over and over, without condemning yourself for having the thoughts in the first place. You'll find that your negative thoughts will slowly fade, leaving a smooth running stream or a calm sky in their place to symbolize your blank mind at rest.

Patrick Fanning, author of *Visualization for Change,* an excellent step-by-step guide to using your powers of imagination for self-improvement, includes a section on obsessive ruminations in his insomnia chapter. If you find yourself ruminating obsessively, he suggests trying to keep your mind busy with an elaborate but pleasant visualization. Imagine conducting an orchestra in your favorite piece of music, watching your favorite sports team play a game, choreographing a ballet or jazz dance, building a fancy piece of furniture, sewing a coat—any long, positive, engaging process that will distract you from your other train of thought. I find this to be particularly helpful, as one who obsesses frequently, and so I build my next house in my visualization. I go over each room, detail by detail. If I find I have reached the end of the imagery (I'm out the back door gazing up at my mansion and am still not asleep), then I go back and start over again, this time picking out colors for each room.

Remember not to criticize your choice of images. Let them flow freely, and with practice you'll find that they become richer and more vivid. Incorporate into your trance an image of yourself sleeping successfully throughout the night, awakening alert and refreshed in the morning. See yourself as confident and in control of your situation. See yourself following the suggestions in this book with dedicated intention. See yourself as successful, and you will be.

Further Reading

Alman, Brian. *Self-Hypnosis: A Complete Manual for Health and Self-Change*. San Diego, Ca.: International Health Publications, 1983.

Fanning, Patrick. *Visualization for Change*. Oakland, Ca.: New Harbinger Publications, Inc, 1988.

Hadley, Josie; Carol Staudacher. *Hypnosis for Change, Second Edition*. Oakland, Ca.: New Harbinger Publications, Inc. 1989.

8

Managing Obsessions

A common lament heard by poor sleepers is "I can't sleep!" Obviously they are lamenting the immediate inability to fall asleep, but there is a hidden message in the phrase "I can't sleep!" That message is one of hopelessness, despair, inability to *ever* make anything right. In other words, "I can't make it right." "I can't sleep!" has a helpless certainty to it that defies flexibility and openness to challenge. Out of frustration and anxiety, the utterer of this phrase not only can't sleep but *won't* sleep.

Insomniacs have a fine ability to obsess. They take this tendency to bed and lie there ruminating about their own and others' shortcomings. For example, rather than move away from anger to problem solving, insomniacs will replay the situation that caused them such anger, over and over. Or, they will endlessly count the ways they, or others, are imperfect.

An underlying issue of any illness or physical disorder is the thought process you bring to the situation. With physical pain, how you think about your pain determines your ability to cope with it. If chronic insomniacs think in a negative way about ever sleeping better, their prophecies will become self-fulfilling. If you find yourself thinking "I'll never get better," "This shouldn't have happened to me," "I'm so embarrassed that I have this problem; I must be less of a person," then you are doing yourself a disservice. You are predetermining that you will never improve.

This chapter is about your thought processes and how they affect your ability to cope with insomnia. Before you give in to the temptation to skip over this chapter and move on to the next one (saying this "doesn't apply to me"), keep an open mind and read on. Don't dismiss your mind's ability to affect your body and blame everything on external stress or a physical ailment. Your mind is a powerful tool that can work to keep you awake all night, or that can be harnessed to help you cope more effectively and sleep.

Obsessional Characteristics of Insomniacs

Studies show that insomniacs tend to be anxious, stressed, and prone to perfectionistic tendencies. Failure is difficult for them to accept, in their own or in others' behavior. Consequently, when others are sleeping peacefully, they lie in bed re-running the day's events, wishing they had said or done something else, trying to avert future catastrophes, and so on.

Insomniacs tend to be physically tense people—they tighten muscles automatically in response to excitement. In turn, they are physically prone to illness and other complaints such as headaches, digestive difficulties, muscular aches, and poor circulation. These symptoms of physical stress all have detrimental sleep effects. Insomniacs also tend toward rigidity and inflexibility. When things do not happen as they "should," or in precise order, insomniacs tense up and dwell on the problem obsessively. They obsess about mistakes, problems, plans, and future uncertainties. If you suspect that you fall into any of these categories, you are probably familiar with the following typical pattern: as you experience difficulty falling asleep, you begin to be concerned about losing sleep. You say to yourself things like: "Oh, no ... not again." Or, "Here I go again. How can I keep doing this?" Or, "I won't be alert for the meeting tomorrow."

These initial thoughts set up a chain reaction. You tense up in response to these negative thoughts, which then makes it harder to relax enough to go to sleep. You may say to yourself "I must go to sleep." Or, "I should try harder," which only sets you up for feelings of failure when you don't perform. You may notice that you can fall asleep much more easily when you're not trying, such as when you're watching TV. High expectations of self are typical of the insomniac. You expect perfection of yourself in every aspect, which leaves no room for the weakness of not being able to sleep on command.

To sum it all up, see if you can spot yourself in the following eight general characteristics of insomniacs:

1. **You have a history of general physical arousal.** Your body becomes tensed and you typically react with stress to excitement, both negative and positive.

2. **You have a specific tendency towards high muscle tension under stress.** You clench your teeth and tighten muscles, which may bring on tension headaches, back pain, fatigue, and general muscular aches.

3. **You have a fear of failure.** The notion of failing at anything is totally unacceptable to you.

4. **You suffer from perfectionistic tendencies.** You cannot allow yourself to be less than perfect, which means you "fail" when you don't sleep well.

5. **You are angry.** You carry anger with you to the bedroom. The anger affects not only your sleep, but your work and home relationships.

6. **You tend to catastrophize.** Your fear of failing and your perfectionistic standards combine to put you constantly on the defensive. You expect the worst to come true of most things and people around you, and worry about what you'll do when it does.

7. **You have a fear of letting go.** This means that you cannot let down your guard, for fear that events and people will escape your control. You must remain ever-vigilant.

8. **You obsess.** Because of your tendencies towards all of the above, you dwell on problems and issues, trying to solve them by incessant worrying.

Steps You Can Take to Counteract Negative, Obsessional Thinking

Step 1: AWARENESS

Even if negative, obsessional thinking impedes your progress towards better sleep, you can take steps to harness that thinking and change it into something that works for you, rather than against you. Your first step is to become aware of your own patterns of obsessional thinking. For one full week, as you drop off to sleep, have paper and pencil by your bedside. You might also have a flashlight handy so as not to disturb your bed-mate. As you notice obsessional thoughts creeping into your mind, jot them down. You can use the following shorthand to label each brand of thinking:

FAIL   — fear of failing
PERF   — tendency towards perfectionism
ANGER — general anger
CATA   — expecting the worst, "what ifs"
GO   — inability to let things go
OBSESS — constant worrying

After one full week, review your notes. Which brand of obsessional thinking do you do the most?

Generally, insomniacs begin to obsess *before* bedtime. Take the second week to jot down your negative obsessional thoughts just before bedtime. You may find it handy to use the sleep diary form you will find in Chapter 3. Or, buy a small notebook to use exclusively to chart your sleep progress. You may find that you have many other types of thoughts that do not fit neatly into the categories provided here. Simply write them down in your own words and become familiar with them. The purpose is to provide yourself a framework within which to work, so that the prospect of controlling negative thinking does not seem overwhelming.

Step 2: COUNTERACT: Stop Your Thoughts

After you feel that you are more fully aware of your style of obsessional thinking, you can begin to counteract each thought. Negative thinking arrives with such spontaneity and fury that you will need to arm yourself with as much counter-ammunition as possible. The ammunition will take the form of positive thoughts delivered with equal force and significance.

Steps to Thought-Stopping As soon as you notice that you are obsessing negatively, choose a way to halt the unproductive flow of thinking abruptly. Some people find that shouting "STOP!" works best, while others raise a hand, snap their fingers, or snap a rubber band around their wrist. Before long, you will have conditioned yourself to recognize and avoid the negative thoughts that bring shock ("STOP!") or pain (a rubber band snapping). You can then fill the void left by the interrupted thought with a previously prepared positive thought. The new thought will be realistic, assertive, and constructive. As soon as you've shouted "STOP," let your mind empty of every trace of the distressing thought, but allow any neutral or pleasant thought to continue. Try to keep your mind blank or on neutral topics for about 30 seconds. If the upsetting thought recurs within 30 seconds, shout "STOP!" again. Keep doing this until you have successfully extinguished the thought. Your focus will be on the word "STOP" if anything.

Once you can completely interrupt the thought by shouting, start saying "STOP" in a normal tone of voice. Practice this until it is just as effective as shouting. Then you will be ready to whisper, or even subvocalize the word STOP, with the same effect. When you master this you can interrupt thoughts covertly, at any place or time without drawing attention to yourself.

It will also help if you remember to breathe deeply and in a relaxed manner at the conclusion of every STOP sequence. The relaxation that deep breathing brings will cue the way for you to accept the positive thoughts you substitute for the negative ones.

The following statements are designed to replace each negative thought. Read them over thoroughly. You may not agree with them at first. This is natural and perfectly acceptable. However, in order for you not to continually lose sleep because you obsess, you will need to find an agreeable replacement, a statement in which you can believe. The counteracting statements that follow are just examples. You may find that you get the best results from developing your own healthy rejoinders to the negative thoughts. Blank lines are available under each counteracting statement for you to write in your own.

Examples of Counteracting Statements
1. When feel yourself tensing up, say to yourself:
    *   "I can relax."
    *   "My muscles are becoming limp."
    *   "I am calmer."
    *   "Breathe deeply."
    my suggestions: _____

    _____

Follow the directions in Chapter 6, *Relaxation for Sleep,* for more instructions on relaxation strategies.

2. Fear of failing:
    *   Think out in advance examples of successes. When obsessing on failures at night, shift focus to an example of success and say to yourself, "Sometimes I succeed, sometimes I don't. Time to relax and sleep."
    *   "I am not a failure."
    *   "I have succeeded in life before."
    *   "Just because I can't sleep tonight doesn't mean I'm a failure."
    *   "I will not suffer tomorrow if I lose sleep to-night."
    my suggestions: _____

    _____

3. Perfectionism:
    *   "It's OK to be less than perfect."

- "No one says I have to be perfect."
- "There is no such thing as a perfect person, and if there were, that person would be very boring."
- "Enough kicking myself for one night. Things may look different in the morning."

my suggestions: _____

_____

4. Anger:
   - "I will leave my anger outside of the bedroom."
   - "All these things making me angry will be waiting for me tomorrow. I can deal with them then."
   - "Let go of angry thoughts. Time to relax."

my suggestions : _____

_____

5. Catastrophizing:
   - "It's impossible that everything will work out for the worst."
   - "Things will be the same whether I worry or not."
   - "Other people have their own issues—they are not out to get me."
   - "Everything seems worse in the middle of the night."

my suggestions: _____

_____

6. Letting Go:
   - "I am learning not to have to control everything."
   - "Stay flexible. I've done what I can; the rest is up to fate."

- "Let it go."

my suggestions: _____

_____

7. Obsessing:
    - "I will counteract each negative thought with a peaceful, soothing thought."
    - "I will not let these thoughts drive me crazy."
    - "I will dismiss them one by one, and replace them with thoughts that will make me sleepy."
    - "I see my negative thoughts floating like autumn leaves on the surface of a stream, drifting around the bend and out of sight.

my suggestions:_____

_____

Replacing your negative thinking takes time, patience, practice, and COMMITMENT. Don't give up if you don't notice immediate improvement in sleep onset and quality. You've spent a lifetime collecting your own unique brand of negative thought; allow yourself time to unravel it and develop better habits.

You will find that using visualization to augment your thinking can add power to your positive thoughts. For example, as you repeat the positive thoughts, visualize yourself as a powerful, confident, and relaxed person. See yourself speaking assertively. Imagine yourself cool under pressure. Recreate feelings of pleasure at your success at staying cool, assertive, and confident. If this is not possible, you may want to choose a positive scene or object, one that evokes feelings of peace and calm. Please refer to Chapter 7, *Self Hypnosis and Imagery,* for more information on visualization.

An Additional Note

This technique of replacing negative thoughts can work at any time, day or night, whenever you notice yourself becoming anxious and full of worries. All you have to do is practice enough, and it will become second nature to react positively rather than negatively. A particularly vulnerable time of the night is in the pre-dawn hours—3 to 5 a.m.—when it's easy to feel overtaken by anxious thoughts. If you awaken frequently during these hours and have difficulty getting back to sleep, prepare yourself before you go to bed each night to administer positive phrases to yourself as soon as necessary.

9

Conditioning Insomnia

Your body responds best to a regular, daily routine. But in modern society there are many temptations to skip routine. It used to be that people went to sleep when it got dark; the regular cycles of night and day routinized their sleep schedules. Now there is good quality lighting available for reading or working. Television offers an endless supply of visual, often mindless distraction. Social changes have had as much impact as technological changes. For instance, interest, education, and economic necessity have merged to encourage many women to work full time outside of the home. Late nights may be the only hours available to catch up on household matters, or to spend concentrated time with family members. Regardless of gender, being "perfect" is still a goal in success-oriented America. For too many people, that means sacrificing sleep in an effort to get there.

Aside from cutting into sleeping hours, all this late night activity may wake you up rather than calm you down enough to go to sleep. In your efforts to be a perfect person, do you find yourself memorizing things you have to do the next day while lying in bed? This is a common example of inappropriately using your bed as an "activity center," or a place where wakeful things are going on that are incompatible with sleepiness. Examples of other incompatible nighttime behaviors in the bed or the bedroom are:

arguing	exercising
lively discussion	cleaning
eating	worrying
reading exciting books	talking on the phone
watching TV	

An athlete conditions his or her body through regular training. He or she works to establish positive habits towards a greater goal. But negative patterns or habits can be learned too. Insomnia can be "conditioned" through associations you develop either consciously or unconsciously. Although you may enjoy the change of pace of a spontaneous late night movie or intimate discussion, be aware that if you repeatedly encourage poor habits, you may unwittingly invite insomnia. Instead, you can train your body, much as an athlete does, to respond to certain cues and adopt specific habits to help you perform better. This chapter helps you look at destructive associations you may make and suggests ways for you to decondition those associations.

Your pre-bed ritual can contain very powerful associations that cue sleepiness. Brushing your teeth, setting the clock, arranging the covers: all can signal sleep time. However, if you associate your bed with stimulating activities such as eating, arguing, or watching TV—sex activity excepted—you may actually have trained yourself to be wakeful rather than sleepy.

For example, one business executive finds herself running through the next day's activities each night before she forces her eyes shut. She begins to dread her bed, because she associates it with a time for mental rehearsal. Her planning and worrying only remind her of unaccomplished tasks, and thus of her imperfections. Another scenario: a freelance artist uses the quiet night to write. She takes restful but lengthy naps to compensate for lost sleep. After a time, she finds that the slant of the late afternoon sun "cues" her naptime. When she's ready to return to a steady job, it's exceedingly difficult to reprogram her body to do without the nap. In both examples certain stimuli (anxious thoughts; naps in the sun) cue certain behaviors (difficulty adapting to "normal" sleep patterns. As time passes, those behaviors prove increasingly ingrained and destructive.

In 1972, a psychologist named Dr. Richard Bootzin pioneered work in stimulus control for insomnia. The above issues are just the ones he considered: what cues are established prior to sleepiness and surrounding the sleep area? Dr. Bootzin determined that a primary goal for the insomnia sufferer is to associate the bed *solely* with sleep, nothing else. The idea makes sense when you consider the many insomniacs who dread their bed because they see it as a place to toss, turn, and worry—and who then find that their sleep is better when they travel, or even move into a different room. In a new setting, their typical non-sleep cues are absent, and they sleep peacefully.

The cornerstone of stimulus control treatment for insomnia is working to create a "new" setting of your own bed. You want it to be associated solely and clearly with restful sleep. This means methodically eliminating all negative associations. The following guidelines, based on Dr. Bootzin's recommendations, will help you achieve this goal.

1. Go to bed *only* when you feel sleepy. If you go to bed too early and then toss and turn, you will experience those very feelings of frustration you want to avoid.

2. Do not use your bed as an activity center. Sexual activity is the only exception. For a list of examples of inappropriate activities, see the first page of this chapter.

3. If you do not fall asleep in about 10 minutes, get out of bed and go into another room. Do a non-arousing activity until you feel sleepy. Only when you feel drowsy should you go back to bed.

4. If *again* you do not fall asleep in about 10 minutes, get up; repeat your non-arousing activity or try another one. Do not return to bed until you feel sleepy.

5. Repeat as often as necessary until you fall asleep within 10 minutes. Your goal is to associate your bed with falling asleep QUICKLY.

6. Get up the same time each morning, regardless of how little you slept. This is a very important step. A consistent uptime will help your body begin to develop a regular sleep rhythm. Resist the temptation to break conditioning by sleeping late on weekend mornings.

7. Do not nap. Your goal is to establish consistent sleep cues at regular times; napping can disrupt your sleep cues.

8. If all else fails, try sleeping in a different room or moving your bed to a different location in your room.

Common Obstacles to This Approach. At first it will feel uncomfortable to jump in and out of bed throughout the night. You may resist leaving a warm bed, especially on cold winter nights. Or you may resent the loneliness of a dark, quiet house. You may even feel particularly fatigued and sluggish for the first few days of trying this approach. Some people complain that they feel even *worse* than usual at the start of this strategy.

These reactions are common and understandable. But be assured that this process has been used successfully for many patients over many years, and has helped chronic insomniacs reshape attitudes towards their beds and sleep. Dr. Bootzin found that 57 percent of the patients in one study who learned this stimulus control training eventually averaged less than 25 minutes a night to fall asleep. This is impressive success rate, especially when compared to a 29 percent "success" for those who used Progressive Muscle Relaxation, 27 percent for those who relied on self relaxation techniques, and 22 percent for the control subjects who received no treatment. Although it is wise for you not to expect immediate improvement, some people have found that they are able to sleep better within a week of carefully following stimulus control techniques. With consistent effort you will find that the sleep you gain in the long run will more than compensate for the sleep you lose those first few nights.

After working with Dr. Bootzin's stimulus control program for some time, another researcher developed a list of suggestions that helped her patients succeed in the program. Dr. Patricia Lacks, of St. Louis, Mo., led patients through the stimulus control treatment plan over a four-week period, within the context of a support group. The list below includes those strategies the group found to be most helpful.

Suggestions for Success

1. While up at night, avoid any activities that might promote alertness. Examples might be having to finish a novel or movie to see how it ends, or doing work brought home from the office. Choose something that can be easily discontinued after two minutes, 15 minutes, or two hours—whenever you feel sleepy. For ideas on mundane things to do, see Chapter 10.

2. Avoid unconsciously "punishing" yourself for not sleeping by forcing yourself to do an unpleasant activity. It will be much harder to get out of the bed if you think you have to face the laundry or the unbalanced checkbook.

3. Make it easier on yourself to get out of bed if you have to by leaving a warm bathrobe and flashlight by your bed. This way you can slip out without disturbing your partner. The house will also seem less dark, cold, and unfriendly.

4. Avoid eating. If you must snack, eat a light food containing carbohydrates or dairy products. Do *not* indulge in sugar, alcohol, caffeine, or any other stimulating foods.

5. Don't worry about following the 10-minute rule to the precise second. Estimate the 10-minute period. The point is, if you find yourself lying in bed fully awake after a reasonable amount of time, get up. But if you estimate that it's been 20 minutes and you feel yourself dropping off to sleep, stay there. Avoid clock-watching.

6. Tell yourself to get up when the alarm clock rings, no matter how restless your night has been. This

is an important step. Remember, you want to re-regulate your internal associations and settle your body into a steady rhythm.

7. Record your progress with conditioning your insomnia on the next day's sleep diary. Keeping a careful record of your sleep progress and behavior will help you gain perspective on your problem. You may spot patterns or connections you had not noticed before. Also, you'll feel a sense of mastery and hope as you see yourself making progress. For a sample diary, see the end of Chapter 3.

You will need to be diligent in following all of the above guidelines in order to break the vicious cycle of your negative associations. But pace yourself; do not expect miracles overnight. Allow yourself time to gradually comprehend and adopt the principles you find in this chapter. If you find that this technique does not work for you, don't panic. Clinicians are not unanimous in their assessment of the success of this technique. You may be one of those people who prefers to adopt one of the other techniques found in this book, such as meditation or gradual muscle relaxation. In any case, making use of the sleep diary in Chapter 3 will help coordinate your plan of action. Share it with a trusted friend or a health care professional. Ask them for support and encouragement. Success can be sweeter when shared with another who supports your accomplishments.

Further Reading

The American Medical Association. *Better Sleep*. New York: Random House, 1984.

Bootzin, R.R.; P.M. Nicassio,"Behavioral Treatments for Insomnia." In M.M. Hersen, et al. (eds.), *Progress in Behavior Modification*, Vol. 6. New York: Academic Press, 1978.

Lacks, Patricia. *Behavioral Treatment for Persistent Insomnia*. New York: Pergamon Press, 1987.

10

The Ten Most Boring Things To Do While Awake*

*Plus Four Bonus Options

If you faithfully follow the stimulus control procedures outlined in the previous chapter, you will at first find yourself sitting up, staring at the walls, and wondering what to do. When this happens, it's a good idea to have a plan. If you organize two or three things you can do while awake, the prospect of getting out of bed won't be so distasteful. You'll have something to look forward to. Of course, you don't want to do anything *too* interesting or stimulating, since the idea is to lull yourself back to sleep.

Ideal activities are those you can begin and end as you choose, so that when you feel sleepy you can put what you're doing aside and go back to bed. A book of short stories might be perfect for you. An activity to *avoid* would be an exciting movie that you just *have* to see to the end. Since a common trait among insomniacs is obsessiveness and compulsiveness, be aware of your tendency to want to complete your projects perfectly. Avoid becoming anxious about your nighttime activities. Carefully choose projects that will help you slow down, not speed up.

One insomnia researcher, Dr. Michael Colligan, wrote in *Creative Insomnia* that when faced with time to kill, you may as well consider it "found" time and enjoy it. He offers lists of things to do, ranging from star gazing to figuring your biorhythms. With his suggestions and the help of a video expert named Tom Wiener, I have put together a suggested list of the *Ten Most Boring Things to Do While Awake*. (At least it started at 10; we were additionally inspired.) These are only suggestions; as you read through them, keep in mind that they may trigger your own unique ideas.

You will note that item 13 on the list is not really very boring. In fact, it involves being quite active, and I included it here because I thought it to be a very creative way to use the nighttime hours. If I could stay awake at night I would definitely do it.

1. Reading: *Fifteen Most Boring Classics, compiled in the* Book of Lists *from a Columbia University survey.*

1. *Pilgrim's Progress*, by John Bunyan
2. *Moby Dick*, by Herman Melville
3. *Paradise Lost*, by John Milton
4. *The Faerie Queene*, by Edmund Spenser
5. *Life of Samuel Johnson*, by James Boswell
6. *Pamela*, by Samuel Richardson
7. *Silas Marner*, by George Eliot
8. *Ivanhoe*, by Sir Walter Scott
9. *Don Quixote*, by Miguel de Cervantes
10. *Faust*, by Johann Wolfgang von Goethe

11. *War and Peace*, by Leo Tolstoy
12. *Remembrance of Things Past*, by Marcel Proust
13. *Das Kapital*, by Karl Marx
14. *Vanity Fair*, by William Makepeace Thackeray
15. *The Mill on the Floss*, by George Eliot

2. Viewing: *Ten Most Boring Movies, compiled by Tom Wiener, author of* The Book of Video Lists.

The first list includes Tom Wiener's opinion of the 10 most boring *and bad* movies. The second list is Tom's collection of movies that are slow moving, boring to him, but may be ultimately rewarding to others. They tend to be quiet, with not much dialogue and/or action. As Tom says, "interesting to some, but real yawners to others." Experiment with the effects of a movie from each list. You may find the first list of bad movies too arousing because they are so bad. On the other hand, they may be perfect for helping you lose interest quickly. If you do not happen to get sleepy watching a movie from the second list, then at least you may have found an intriguing movie for a better occasion.

Boring and Bad (not necessarily in order of boringness)
1. *The Appaloosa*
2. *Changes*
3. *Endless Love*
4. *Executive Action*
5. *The Island*
6. *Quintet*
7. *A Separate Peace*
8. *Superman III*
9. *True Stories*
10. *Welcome to L.A.*

optional: *Day of the Dolphin*

Slow Movers
1. Most Michelangelo Antonioni movies, for example *L'Avventura*.
2. Most Eric Rohmer movies, for example *My Night at Maud's*.
3. Stanley Kubrick's *Barry Lyndon*.
4. *Stranger Than Paradise*
5. *Persona*
6. *Paris, Texas*
7. *My Dinner With Andre*
8. Andy Warhol's Trilogy: *Flesh, Trash,* and *Heat*

3. Collect, cut, and organize coupons.

If you like saving grocery money by using coupons, take the nighttime to throw out expired ones and organize the current ones. Put them into food groups. Devise a coupon holder so that they stay neat and retrievable.

4. Organize your recipe box.

How many times have you gone thumbing through your recipe box searching for that out of place recipe while the water's boiling over and your hands are full of eggplant? Here's a perfect opportunity to once-and-for-all throw out those recipes you *will NEVER* use and put into order those you will. Rewrite well-loved recipes that are now splattered and stained. Put clear protective tape over those you plan to use regularly. Or, put them behind plastic or in a photo album for protection and easy location.

5. Remove your name from the junk mail lists.

Always a wish of many people, but unfortunately low on the priority list. Here's your chance to make it clear to money-grubbing vendors that you do not want their paper stuffing your mailbox. Do one or all of the following:

    a. Write to magazines you subscribe to. Ask them *not* to disclose your name or address to other services. This is the number 1 way your name gets out.

    b. Collect all junk mail for one or two months. Systematically write to each and every vendor requesting that they remove your name from their list.

    c. Get a copy of Form 2150 from the U.S. Postal Service and list all the vendors on the form. The post office will pull the mail before it is delivered.

    d. Write to Direct Mail/Marketing Association, Inc., 6 East 43rd St., New York, NY, 10017. Ask for their "Mail Preference Service Form." This group is the professional association for junk mailers. They will take your name off their master list.

6. Organize your phone/address book.

Discard out-dated names. Make sure you have current numbers listed for your doctor(s), pharmacy, fire and police departments, and any other emergency services you might need.

7. Old photographs:

Pull out those years of photos still in their packets from the camera shop and organize them in an album.

8. Take a warm bath. Luxuriate in it.

9. Listen to soothing music.

There are literally hundreds of audio cassette tapes available that specialize in "soothing sounds." You have a wide variety of choices ranging from ocean waves to "space" music for a new age. For example, Moodtapes has videos, cassettes, laser discs, and compact discs designed to tranquilize—or energize—you "naturally." Write to 3960 Laurel Canyon Blvd., Suite 221, Studio City, Ca, 91604, for a catalogue. In California call 800-342-4552; outside California call 800-451-4571.

10. Take up needlepoint, quilting, knitting, etc.

Once you get the hang of it, these activities require very little active attention and can provide hours of distraction. If you still need to satisfy that compulsive part of you and don't want to take up anything new until you finish old work, then get into mending clothes.

11. Computer games.

Some people say these are a relaxing distraction. For example, there are several programs available to play computer chess for under $50.00, but be warned that this may become more stimulating than you think. *Sargon III* is a popular chess game; write to Hayden Software Company, 600 Suffolk St., Lowell, Ma, 01854.

12. Begin your own list of "Ten Most Boring Things To Do."

And send them to me, c/o New Harbinger Publications, 5674 Shattuck Ave., Oakland, Ca, 94609.

13. Travel to Baltimore, Md to participate in one of their Insomnia Tours.

Once or twice a year, Baltimore Rent-A-Tour conducts very popular insomnia tours for night-owl fun. Beginning at 1:30 a.m., the tours visit a variety of historic and cultural sights and wind up with a post-sunrise breakfast. A great way to beat the traffic! Baltimore Rent-A-Tour might consider organizing an insomnia tour in your area. Call or write Ruth Fader, Baltimore Rent-A-Tour, 3414 Philips Drive, Baltimore, Md, 21208, 301-653-2998.

14. Optional boring thing to do.

Do your taxes. Guaranteed to induce sleep and/or infuriation.

Hopefully these ideas have stimulated your thinking, and you now have a plan to keep yourself occupied. Perhaps these things are so BORING that you'd just as soon go back to sleep. In any case, know that you have options. Keep a positive attitude when you can't sleep. Consider these "extra" hours an opportunity to read that (mildly boring) book you've always wanted to read, or begin that knitting project. Staying positive and up-beat is better than being fretful. It's less stressful and much more productive.

Further Reading

Colligan, Douglas. *Creative Insomnia.* New York: Franklin Watts, 1978.

Weiner, Tom. *The Book of Video Lists.* Lanham, Md: Madison Books, 1988.

11

Circadian Rhythms and Sleep

The word *circadian* is composed of the Latin words *circa* (about) and *dies* (day): it means "about a day." In the 1940s and '50s, researchers strove to determine human sleeping and waking cycles around the clock. These cycles came to be known as circadian cycles or rhythms. Dr. Nathaniel Kleitman, often called the father of modern sleep research, once stated that sleep is "part of a perpetual cycle and the most powerful organizer of our lives." When you fall out of sync with your body's natural, daily cycle, you and your day feel disrupted.

Your daily rhythms are synchronized with your body's internal and external cues. The primary internal cue is your inner "body clock," which regulates certain physiological functions such as body temperature and hormone levels. A body clock is one way to picture the control of the circadian rhythm. Examples of other bodily functions that reflect cyclic changes are heart rate, blood pressure, endocrine secretions, metabolism, breathing, and associated mood swings.

External cues include the amount of sunlight available and the "social clock," or daily activities such as mealtimes. If time is distorted, as when you travel across time zones or are forced to lose sleep, your body's rhythm falls out of sync with its environment. The results can be very unsettling: difficulty falling asleep, restless and disturbed sleep, and fatigue and disorientation the following day.

Common causes of circadian rhythm disruption are:

1. Insomnia due to self-imposed sleep-wake schedule disruption. An example might be a student cramming for exams and limiting sleep to naps or to hourly increments.
2. Insomnia related to shift work or night work.
3. Rapid time zone change syndrome, also known as "jet lag," and sometimes referred to as "transmeridian travel sleep disorder."

Your Internal Time Clock

Human circadian rhythm in individuals can vary from 24 to 28 hours, with a general average around 25 hours. This means that if you were left to your own free will, without any external stimuli such as changes from night to day or alarm clocks, your circadian rhythm would adapt to a roughly 25-hour schedule. During this cycle your body temperature rises and falls in a predictable cycle, which in turn affects when you feel sleepy and when you are ready to be awake and alert. Since the inherent human rhythm is a little longer than the 24-hour day, people instinctively gravitate towards going to bed an hour later and getting up an hour later each day. This has an impact on your ability to adapt to work shift and time zone changes, as you will see later in this chapter.

Body temperature fluctuations account for dips and peaks in mental and physical alertness. Temperatures generally are lowest during the latter half of sleep, about 3 a.m. to 5 a.m., when most people least need to be alert because they're most deeply asleep. Temperatures rise in the morning, peaking somewhere between midday and the late afternoon, and begin to fall as the evening hours approach. However, there is a great deal of individual variation in the precise times that people peak during the day. This may explain why some people are morning people, or "larks," and others are night people, or "owls." Larks' temperatures tend to peak earlier than owls'. Dr. Kleitman discovered that alertness follows body temperature: you feel most alert and perform best when body temperature is highest, and least alert when body temperature is lowest. Of course, external factors can affect these dips and peaks, such as extreme hot or cold climates, eating and drinking hot or cold foods, and vigorous exercise. And, no matter if you're an owl or lark, it seems that everyone is affected by the familiar phenomenon of "post-lunch dip." This occurs in most adults around 2 p.m., and may be a secondary circadian subrhythm having nothing to do with the amount of lunch you've eaten!

Society expects its members to conform to a 24-hour cycle, which is usually not a tremendous problem for most people. However, you may notice that on weekends you tend to go to bed later and get up later, so that by Monday morning you are slightly out of sync with your usual Monday rising time. This is the mark of that natural drift towards later bedtimes and uptimes mentioned earlier. You may simply notice that after a day or two of working days you are back on your regular schedule, feeling rested and alert when you awaken.

Some people, however, have serious difficulty adjusting to a 24-hour cycle. Owls, for example, really don't feel awake until the late afternoon hours. They reach their peak alertness sometime in the late evening, when larks are yawning and getting ready for bed. In contrast, larks feel that their best hours are in the first half of the day; they usually have a low period in the afternoon and then are truly ready for sleep between 9 and 11 p.m. Some theories hold that larks tend to be introverted people, and owls extroverts! (That may just reveal owls' penchant for late-night parties!)

One freelance artist felt that she produced her best work in the evening hours. She developed the habit of watching late night TV to relax after an evening's work. However, her spouse's alarm clock went off at the same early hour each morning. To compensate, she woke up late and took restful but lengthy naps in the afternoon. She found it increasingly difficult to go to sleep at a regular hour with her spouse. The artist has a stimulus control problem such as that discussed in Chapter 9—her daytime ritual involved a nap and her pre-bed ritual involved late night TV. Combined with these cues, she also fell into her natural circadian rhythm by allowing herself to go to sleep later and later. In order to get back on a schedule more like her spouse's, she needed to reset her body's clock.

If you choose a family lifestyle and a career that allow you to work at your own rhythm and pace, sleep-wake schedules may not be an issue. But if you suspect that part of your insomnia is due to unsynchronized schedules, you may want to discuss this problem further with a specialist at a sleep lab. Sometimes known as "chronotherapists," these specialists can carefully examine your individual sleep-wake schedule and help you find alternative solutions.

You can also take the Owl and Lark Questionnaire at the end of Chapter 3 to determine your preference if you don't already know for sure. You may decide, based on the results of the questionnaire and after reading the next section, that you can adapt more easily than you thought to night shift work. Or you may decide that you are better off on a typical daytime schedule.

Shift Work Syndrome

Many Americans work night shifts and/or rotating shifts. It is estimated that as many as 36 percent of all American males and 26 percent of all American females hold jobs with a "variable" work schedule, which includes occasional night work, according to a 1985 National Center of Health Statistics survey. Due to the constantly increasing needs of competitive industry, incentives are given to employees—increased salaries, bonuses, and other advantages—to keep the factories operating at peak around the clock. But little attention is paid to whether workers themselves can operate at peak around the clock. "Most existing work schedules are incompatible with the properties of the human circadian time system," write Drs. Charles Czeisler and James Allan of Harvard Medical School. While working rotating shifts does have advantages, there is a high rate of reported sleep complaints in shift workers.

A few of the advantages, besides increased pay, are that shift workers don't have to face the traffic and shopping congestion of normal working hours, and they may have significantly more autonomy on evening or night shifts. But many studies claim greater physical ailments among rotating shift workers. In addition, researchers have found the personal injury rate of rotating shift workers to be two to three times greater than that of permanent day, evening, or night workers. Shift workers also complain of:

- Irregular eating habits, poor diet
- Disorientation
- Fatigue, anxiety
- Strained family relationships
- Low morale among co-workers
- Absenteeism
- Inability to participate in hobbies or exercise

One expert in this field, Dr. Richard Coleman of Stanford University Medical School, has consulted with many businesses about creative adaptation of shift work to the human circadian rhythm. Shift work is here to stay, he acknowledges. But certain changes can make it less personally disruptive, such as rotating shifts in a clockwise fashion: from days to evenings to nights. This way workers can follow the natural lengthening of their day, based on the average 25-hour cycle. If you went the other way—counterclockwise—you would be cutting back an hour or two each day. Imagine trying to fall asleep earlier, for example by 7 p.m., if your normal bedtime is 11 p.m. You would be fueling sleep onset difficulties.

Dr. Coleman further suggests that shifts last three weeks instead of one. If the rotation period is once a week, shiftworkers never have a chance to adapt to a new rhythm.

Studies show that when companies adapt shifts to accommodate human circadian rhythms and worker comfort levels, there is a marked improvement in employee health and performance. Some companies have adopted a "rapid rotation" system, where the shifts are one day, one evening, and one night in a row. In this way the worker does not spend enough time on any one shift to adapt to that shift, and remains primarily on daytime rhythm.

You may choose to be permanently assigned to one shift, such as the night shift. The only problem with a fixed shift is that you still need adjustment time when you revert back to everyone else's hours on the weekends. But for the most part you can gradually reset your inner clock to adapt to shift work. In effect you invert the regular sleep-wake schedule so that you are alert at 3 a.m. when others are normally sleepy. Dr. Peter Hauri suggests that in order to reset your internal clock, you choose to shift your cycle to an earlier time frame, forcing yourself to get up when the alarm rings. You cannot force sleepiness, only wakefulness. Rather than trying to go to sleep earlier in order to awaken earlier, go to sleep at your regular time and get less sleep that night. The resulting tiredness will help you fall asleep earlier the next night. Over a period of weeks, you can accomplish a resetting of shifts.

The roughest schedules to adapt to seem to be rotating shifts, where complete adaptation to the new schedule is never made. The human body seems most comfortable working either straight days or straight nights. If you must work rotating shifts, remember that it may take as many as nine full days to adjust. Also, owls and younger people adapt more readily to shift work.

Normal human sleep needs range from three to 10 hours a night. If you are trying to force yourself to get more or less sleep, your body may be trying to tell you something. You may need more or less sleep than you think.

Jet Lag Syndrome

Since people adapt naturally to going to sleep an hour later and rising an hour later each day, it is usually easier to lengthen days rather than shorten them. This may explain why you feel less disruption in your schedule when you add an hour in the fall, compared to losing an hour in the spring. This may also explain why it's less stressful to travel from east to west. Traveling from New York to California makes your day seem longer; this corresponds to your body's natural tendency. But imagine traveling from New York to Paris and arriving at 9 a.m. With a six-hour time difference, the morning arrival in Europe corresponds to the point at which your body temperature is lowest—and you feel the least responsive and alert. You've also shortened your day, fighting against your internal clock.

Dr. Czeisler reports that before people have adapted to a new time zone, there is an increased risk of accidents, errors, and injuries due to decreased alertness. He cites a study done in 1980 by Dr. Timothy Monk, whose research results showed a 10 to 11 percent increase in automobile accidents during the week following the introduction of daylight savings time, "which did not occur in certain years when the change was cancelled to conserve energy." Even if you don't travel cross country, you feel the effects twice a year of a one-hour time difference! The rule of thumb is, for every one-hour time zone you cross, you will need one full day to recover.

The uncomfortable symptoms of jet lag are unforget-table.

- Fatigue, decreased alertness
- Loss of appetite
- Frequent nighttime urination
- Irresistible sleepiness and/or insomnia
- Disorientation/sense of confusion
- Decreased concentration and performance

Frequent flyers, such as airline crews, also report an increase in gastrointestinal disorders and nervousness.

Journeys by ship, bus, or train will *not* have the same effects. Evidently the slower rate of travel allows for adjustment time. You also have to cross time zones to feel the effects of jet lag; traveling from North to South America, for example, produces no symptoms.

Research shows that those who get out of their hotel rooms and adapt as quickly as possible to the new time zone, which includes as much outdoor activity as pos-sible (exposure to light), have less disruption from jet lag. Otherwise, adaptation to the new environment occurs within two days to two weeks.

Suggestions for Overcoming Jet Lag

- Do *not* schedule important meetings immedi-ately upon your arrival; try to arrive a day or two early to recover from jet lag as completely as possible.
- You can choose to stay on home time, especially if you are visiting briefly and are able to control activities.
- Adopt the social activities of the new time zone upon arrival; go outside, eat meals on local

time, stay active, and then turn in earlier. In other words, don't go to your hotel room and go to sleep right away, or you will prolong the adjustment period. Evidence shows that as much exposure to sunlight as possible will aid your adjustment to the new time zone; if you don't feel like walking around, at least sit outside.

- Use a short-acting sleeping pill to help you sleep on the first night at your destination (with your doctor's approval).
- Anticipate the time zone of your destination by adjusting to its mealtimes, activities, and sleep time wherever possible before your trip. For example, if you are traveling east to west, go to bed and get up an hour later each day for three days before your trip. For west to east travel, move sleep time back an hour earlier each day.
- There is not sufficient evidence to prove the claims of a jet lag diet, but some researchers and frequent travelers advocate the following traveler's diet:

    Three to four days before departure, alternate meals of high protein foods, high carbohydrate foods, and fasting type foods. High protein meals might include cereals, eggs, meat, chicken, or fish. High carbohydrate meals include breads, potatoes, or pasta. Fasting foods include soups, salads, fruits, and juices. The theory is that alternating meals, and the timing of those meals, can help induce shifts to the new time zone. Also, a high protein diet is thought to promote alertness and a high carbohydrate diet to stimulate sleep.

Some people are affected more strongly by jet lag than others. Elderly people, for example, have more difficulty adapting to different time zones. Also, it appears that owls adapt more easily to crossing time zones and experience fewer ill effects in general.

Further Reading

The American Medical Association. *Guide to Better Sleep.* New York: Random House, 1984.

Anch, A. Michael; Carl P. Browman; Merrill M. Mitler; James K. Walsh. *Sleep: A Scientific Perspective.* Englewood Cliffs, NJ: Prentice-Hall, 1988.

Coleman, Richard. *Wide Awake at 3:00 A.M., By Choice or by Chance?* New York: W. H. Freeman and Co., 1986.

Dryer, Bernard, M.D.; Ellen Kaplan. *Inside Insomnia.* New York: Villard Books, 1986.

Williams, Robert; Ismet Karacan; Constance Moore; eds. *Sleep Disorders: Diagnosis and Treatment.* 2nd ed. New York: John Wiley and Sons, 1988. (A volume in the Wiley Series in General and Clinical Psychiatry.)

12

Sleep and Dreaming

"Sweet dreams…," people wish warmly to one another before drifting off. For many, however, those words are contradictory. If you experience nightmares, dreams are anything but sweet, and may cause sweating, tossing and turning, and a severe dread of sleep. Nightmares are the most common type of sleep disturbance in adulthood. The problem may be as simple as an occasional annoying dream, or it may be a persistent, devastating nocturnal event.

Some people swear they never dream. But they do. Every single night your brain concocts elaborate plots that are sometimes meaningful, sometimes nonsensical. Your dream plots may fade to the point that, upon awakening, you are unaware you were even dreaming. It is estimated that dreams occur approximately 80% of the time you are in the stage of sleep called rapid eye movement, or REM sleep. REM sleep, so called because the eye rapidly shifts back and forth and up and down during this phase of sleep, occurs about once every 90 minutes in the sleep cycle throughout the night. REM lasts anywhere from 10 to 50 minutes, and there are typically four to six REM periods in a night. That leaves you ample time for dreaming!

REM periods also lengthen as the night wears on, which probably explains why your dreams appear to be so much more vivid and numerous just before you wake up. Dreaming can also occur during the other stages of the sleep cycle, stages 1 through 4, also known as non-REM or NREM sleep. However, these dreams are reported to be more general and vague in nature, with less action and fewer identifiable characters and objects. This probably accounts for the fact that REM dreams are more clearly remembered.

If you dread going to sleep because you fear the return of a bad dream, you will benefit from becoming familiar with and desensitized to your dreams. Using the techniques outlined in this chapter, you can actually gain control over your dreams. You can learn to escape nightmares in the earliest stages and even turn them into learning experiences. Once you have mastered the principles of "lucid dreaming," your dreams can help you unravel daily hassles and deep anxieties that may be contributing to your nightmares.

Why You Dream

Scientists have yet to fully explain the precise reason for dreaming. Some say dreaming is an immense housecleaning effort by the brain, as it chemically sorts out the day's events from past and recent memories—a sort of clearing of the mind's cobwebs. Other researchers credit a random firing of neurons; they say chaotic electrical impulses travel from the brain stem to the cortex (the center of higher reason and vision), which struggles to organize those random impulses by affixing images and plots culled from memory. Over the years, and before technology afforded a view of actual mental activity, others have attached far more complex and exotic philosophies to dreaming.

The ancients often attributed dreams to external sources, although they saw dreams as rich in personal meaning. One of the earliest reportings of dream therapy occurred in Grecian times, hundreds of years B.C., when dream healers used "incubation" temples for dreamers to sleep in and work with their dreams. The Greeks believed that dreams brought messages of hope and healing from the gods. Contrast this to other periods in history when dreams were not regarded in a positive light, but were rather considered evil invaders of the body by the devil and bad gods. Freud, in the early 1900s, was the first to explore the meaning of dreams from a perspective of unconscious impulses. Freud suggested that the body attempted to "act out" its wishes and desires, often sexual, through dreams. Freud's disciple, Jung, attached a more mystical meaning to dreams, choosing to interpret them as symbols of universal human experience.

Modern researches have been drifting towards a behavioral explanation of dreaming. For example, some say that dreaming may be a purely adaptive response, allowing the dreamer to periodically "wake up just a bit" throughout the night to check out the environment. If it is safe, the dreamer can go back to sleep. Richard Coleman of Stanford University Medical School writes in *Wide Awake at 3:00 A.M.* that "REM sleep and dreaming may serve as an adaptational process. The amount of REM sleep of recently divorced women has been shown in recent studies to increase, supporting the theory that dreaming enhances the capacity to cope with emotional problems.

With all the controversy surrounding the origin and purpose of dreaming, two things remain certain:

1. Everyone dreams throughout the night
2. Dreaming reflects upon one's waking state

Researchers have concluded that dream content relates to pre-sleep thinking and tasks. Thinking anxious thoughts and/or doing anxiety-provoking activities before bedtime will likely encourage disturbing dreams. Obsessions and desires that haunt you as you lie down to sleep will often find their way into your dreams. For example, laboratory dreams of patients with anorexia nervosa (an eating disorder) contain oral images and preoccupations with food and drink. Ex-smokers will often report vivid dreams of smoking a cigarette for as long as one year after they quit.

Several other factors complicate dream content, such as physical condition and substance abuse. Some researchers have found an increase in dream anxiety and hostility during the premenstrual and menstrual phases of a woman's monthly cycle. Others have shown that "REM rebound" occurs with withdrawal from substances such as alcohol and some sleeping pills, resulting in frequent and vivid dreams that can seem like nightmares.

It is not surprising that people with vivid and frightening dreams come to dread bedtime. Going to sleep can seem like giving oneself up to forces of evil. But the lucid dreaming techniques described at the end of this chapter can help you regain control over your nights. A series of steps can help you recognize the fact that you are in a dream *while you're still dreaming*—an awareness that alone can ease your fear. With practice you can find a way out of your nightmares, and even turn them into positive learning experiences. As with other sleep disturbances, such as night terrors and sleepwalking, an effective treatment is really a double cure. It eases the problem itself, and removes the resistance to sleep the problem brings on.

Nightmares, Night Terrors, and Sleepwalking

Nightmares, night terrors, and sleepwalking fall into the general category of "parasomnias," or partial arousals throughout the night that disrupt sleep. While night terrors—moments of acute fear or disorientation that are usually forgotten afterwards—and sleepwalking most commonly occur in childhood, nightmares are the most common form of parasomnia in adults. Before looking at nightmares in greater depth, consider the two related disturbances. Night terrors and sleepwalking have been shrouded in greater mystery than nightmares, although research has gone a long way toward demystifying the phenomena. There are clear theories about their causes and effective treatments for their relief.

Night terrors occur in the first part of the night's sleep, usually within one to two hours, during stages 3 or 4, the deepest sleep (sometimes known as Delta sleep). Occurring rarely in adults, the main feature of a night terror is amnesia: that is, remembering nothing or recalling only a brief, frightening image. Sufferers may experience a pressing sensation on the chest or a feeling of invasion, resulting in relatively short episodes of confusion, disorientation, vocal outbursts, and sleepwalking. Dr. Joyce Kales of Pennsylvania State University reports that persons who experience both night terrors and sleepwalking frequently have family

138 Getting to Sleep

histories involving one or the other. Often those who experience night terrors or sleepwalking will encounter the other problem, as well.

Night terrors may occur most often in children due to the underdevelopment of the child's nervous system, explains Dr. Ernest Hartman of Tufts University, Massachusetts. In adults, night terrors definitely increase at times of stress and may worsen if the person is experiencing a great deal of pent up anger.

Night terrors are not to be confused with hypnogogic hallucinations. These bizarre sensations occur right at the point of falling asleep and involve vivid, startling imagery. They can be frightening, but the sensation is quite different from the acute panic and obscure images associated with night terrors.

Some researchers have suggested that sleepwalking, known in medical terms as "somnambulism," is the culmination of a night terror. Sleepwalking affects young and old alike. Since it occurs primarily in the deeper non-REM sleep stages, the sleepwalker rarely talks and does not remember the episode. Still, he or she can be quite active: walking around, using the bathroom, and so forth. The sleepwalker usually cannot be awakened; if an attempt is made, he or she will be disoriented and confused.

Dr. Ismet Karacan of Baylor College in Texas reports that while sleepwalking and night terrors are seen as central nervous system immaturities in children, they are often associated with psychopathology in adults. This does not mean that an adult who sleepwalks is definitely mentally disturbed; rather, studies show a higher incidence of psychological problems in adult sleepwalkers, such as stress, aggressive tendencies, and depression.

Counselling and psychotherapy are recommended as effective strategies for dealing with the underlying emotions contributing to the parasomnias. The benzodiazepine class of drugs, such as diazepam (Valium), may work well to control terrors and sleepwalking since they are found to suppress the deepest stages of sleep, stages 3 and 4, where terrors and sleepwalking occur. Sometimes sleepwalkers can find relief in afternoon naps. Also, hypnosis can be use to cue waking when the person becomes aware of an urge to sleepwalk (see Chapter 7 for more on hypnosis).

If you wake up to find a family member sleepwalking, you are advised to do the following: steer the sleeper back to bed, protecting him or her from injury. Don't try to awaken him or her.

Researchers are still not certain what triggers the development of these parasomnias. One finding is that a strong stress component is involved. For this reason, relaxation techniques can be particularly effective in combatting night terrors and sleepwalking. Deep breathing, systematic muscle relaxation, hypnosis with soothing imagery—all can help put your mind and body at peace, where stressful disturbances are less likely to take hold. Of course, these techniques also help overcome the dread and tension that contribute to your sleep disturbance problem. Refer to Chapters 6 and 7 for directions on specific relaxation and hypnotic techniques.

The most common parasomnia in adults, nightmares, deserves special attention. Researchers know a bit more about this problem than the other sleep disturbances. They have also hit upon a particularly effective and exciting technique for defusing the power of nightmares.

Doctors report that the average time of nightmare occurrence is three and a half hours after sleep onset, typically during the REM cycle of sleep. Since REM periods lengthen and predominate later in the night, it makes sense that nightmares would be more easily remembered than other types of dreams—they are fresher in your mind at waking time.

Nightmares also have a different character than dreams that occur at other times in the night cycle. They tend to be more vivid, complex and full of plots, objects, and characters. Dr. Kales reports that more than 80% of adult nightmare sufferers complain about recurring nightmares, and that the dream content is usually fear of attack or death.

Occasionally, illness brings on nightmares, but for the most part nightmares occur as a result of anxiety-producing events in your life. While you are likely to awaken from a nightmare and realize that you have had one (and stay awake for an average of 25 minutes), it is very difficult to awaken people who are experiencing night terrors and/or sleepwalking; they become extremely confused.

In the remainder of this chapter, you will learn to desensitize yourself to the negative anticipation of dreaming. You can find relief from nightmares by learning to control your dreams with lucid dreaming techniques.

Using Lucid Dreaming to Control Dream Impact

Although guiding and controlling dreams was a hallmark of healing for many ancient peoples, the term "lucidity" was not introduced into modern dream work until the early 1900s. The experience of lucid dreaming has been described by modern writers, doctors, and experimenters—often in glowing terms—since at least the mid-1800s. But only recently has the technique gained wide acceptance as a way to control bad dreams.

As the name suggests, lucid dreaming is a way to make your dreams visible and clear to you: you realize you are in a dream, you decide to change that dream, and you let yourself explore that dream. In a regular dream, the dreamer may not be aware that he or she is dreaming until awakening. That accounts for the power of dreaming: it feels like a real-life experience. In a lucid dream, however, the dreamer can see without waking up that the experience is only a dream. The realization strips the terror from the dream. A lucid dreamer can then enter the dream, take a conscious and active role in it, and direct it away from a frightening or negative ending. He or she can even choose to explore the dream, turning monsters into insightful characters and nightmares into learning experiences.

With lucid dreaming techniques, it is possible to plan in advance to deal with a recurring troublesome dream. For example, suppose you identify a certain character or theme that reappears regularly in your dreams. Perhaps this character or theme is frightening, causing you to wake up in a sweat every night it appears. You can actually arm yourself against this dream situation, planting helpful escape routes and even objects into your waking mind through self-talk and meditation. Better yet, you can decide to find out why a troublesome character is visiting you in your dreams, so that you can resolve its threat and sleep peacefully.

One woman, for example, was bothered repeatedly by a hooded figure who emanated a bright and piercing light. The dreamer would wake up in a panic every time the figure appeared, and toss and turn in bed for a long time from anxiety. She would feel agitated and even embarrassed that this dream figure could be so disturbing. Finally she decided to try to become lucid in the dream so that she could see behind it and find relief. Before falling asleep, she repeated these phrases to herself:

> I will not be afraid when this dreams appears.
> I will realize I am in a dream, and choose not to wake up.
> I will ask what the hooded figure wants.

In just a few nights, she was able to engage the hooded figure in a dialogue. The dreamer saw the blinding light fade, and watched the figure's robe disintegrate to reveal a kindly old gentleman. Once the fear was gone, she was able to go on to explore the meaning of the old man's presence in her dream.

The three principles of lucid dreaming—knowing you're in a dream, choosing to change that dream, and choosing to explore that dream—can be learned by almost anybody with practice. In fact, some estimates have it that more than half of all adult men and women experience a spontaneous lucid dream at some point. Bringing the experience on at will takes time, dedication, and the patience and faith to keep on trying. Keep an open mind about the process, even if the steps seem strange or don't seem to make any difference at first. A mere awareness of your dreams and their potentially positive power can help alleviate your dread of sleep, and pave the way for fewer troubling nightmares. Dreams don't need to control you; remember that it is you, and your brain, controlling your dreams. Lucid dreaming will just help make that control more conscious.

Knowing You're in a Dream

The first principle behind lucid dreaming is that you train yourself to be aware of your state of consciousness: waking or sleeping. You want to make this self-awareness such a habit that your dreaming self takes it on, too. A simple way to check your state of consciousness is to look at your hand. Your hand is real and solid and it hurts if you pinch it. Even if it feels strange at first, get into the habit of looking down at your hand and asking yourself "Am I awake or dreaming?" Your solid hand should give you the answer. You can write a small "A" (for awake) on your hand, if it helps you focus on it.

Throughout the day, interrupt your activity for a few seconds each time to ask yourself "Am I awake or dreaming?" Look for the signposts of being awake—the letter "A," or the familiar lines on your hand, or the way your hand feels in the air or on a desk. If you like, an expansion of this technique is to look for signs of dreaming—could you fly if you wanted to? Shrink? Whatever sequence of questions or tests you establish, be sure to repeat them the same way each time. You are trying to establish a habit.

Changing Your Dreams

It can be exhilarating to realize that you can actually change the course of your dreams. After all, that's just what will free you from the horror of your nightmares: you can turn them into neutral, even positive, dreams.

In choosing from the dazzling array of options available to you, there are just a few guidelines to keep in mind. For one thing, it's best not to hope to create a perfect dream. You simply want to work within the dream you find yourself in, to steer it in a positive direction. Think about cooperating, not manipulating. Think about controlling your own actions, not the whole dream.

One way to plan your role in a dream is to arm yourself with the tools you'll need in the dream. Spend some time thinking about your typical dream patterns; start writing in a dream journal so you can remember your dreams, and find similarities among them. You don't need to write down every detail, but try to write something every morning so you get used to capturing the experience of dreaming. If you can identify a particular dream or detail that recurs, ask yourself what change you would like to see in it. Think of a specific plot-twist, action, or helpful object you would like to have in your dream. You can then incorporate vivid images of that change into your pre-bed relaxation ritual. You want to fix the image in your head, and trigger an association between the beginning of the dream and the change you have planned. Run through a version of your typical dream in your head, focusing on the change you want to insert. A few sentences of self-talk as you drift off can help you take that change with you into your dream. "When the muggers chase me around the corner, a policeman or somebody will be there to help me."

Once you have become lucid in a dream (you realize you *are* in a dream), what will you do? Take action. Reason with the monster to go away; look for the escape ladder you know you planted in the room. This is your opportunity to take control. Instead of hoping to change the entire dreamscape, focus in on your own actions. Chances are that once you respond in an aware way to your dream surroundings, the dream itself will change to accommodate you. Maybe the monster will dissolve; maybe it will become a kind person willing to talk to you. Since you'll know you're dreaming, you'll find many more options available to you, and much less reason to fear the thing that threatens you.

Exploring Your Dreams

The final principle of lucid dreaming is that you decide to explore the messages and symbols behind a dream. It's good thing to be able to scare a monster away; it's a better thing to find out *why* the monster is bothering you, *who* the monster could be, and what fear in your daily life the monster might represent. Of course, such questions form the basis of much discussion in a therapist's office. But it can be much more revealing and effective to explore these issues while you are still in your dream. Lucid dreaming allows you that control.

When you confront a frightening dream figure, try to engage it in dialogue. Instead of fleeing, talk. Ask in a friendly voice, "Who are you," or even, "Who am I?" Try to calm an angry figure down by talking instead of fighting. Listen to what it's saying; ask "What do you mean by that?" If the figure still attacks, stare it in the face and let it know you won't back down. Your goal is to achieve a peaceful reconciliation—and to find out someting about the attacker. Since your dream character is really a different part of yourself, the answers you get may give you considerable insight into your own fears and concerns. What's more, once you have de-mystified or decoded a dream figure, it's less likely to come back and haunt your sleep. The awareness and peace you find will probably carry over into your waking life.

Steps to Lucid Dreaming

A. Self-awareness

1. Become aware of your waking state. Ask yourself five times a day "Am I awake or dreaming?" Then look at your hand. You might try writing a small "A" (for awake) on your hand to focus in on. The more you ask this question, the more likely your dreaming self will ask it too.

2. When anything unusual or improbable happens, ask yourself "Am I awake or dreaming?" Look at your hand to see if you are awake. (Or try to shrink, or fly, to see if you are dreaming.)

3. If you are aware of a recurring element in your dreams (such as a cat), ask yourself "Am I awake or dreaming" any time you encounter one.

B. Dream awareness

4. Become aware of your dreams. Keep a dream journal by your bed and every time you wake up write down as much of the dream as you can remember. Don't worry if you can't recall all of the dream; sometimes just getting into the "feeling" of the dream will trigger recall. Dream fragments may be sufficient to piece together the dream action.

5. Practice dream recall. Resolve to remember at least one dream per night.

6. Become familiar with your typical dream content. Do certain patterns emerge? People?

Things? Keep note of these in your dream journal.

7. Think about something specific you would like to change in your dreams. If you have a recurring nightmare, think of something—an object or a plot change—that would help you out of it. Be very specific. A magical ladder might help you out of a locked dream-room, for instance, or a penetrating question might stop a monster in its tracks.

C. Bedtime

8. Take 10 deep breaths when you first go to bed to begin easing tension. Then use your favorite relaxation or meditation technique to become as relaxed and receptive as you can be.

9. Tell yourself as you begin to drift off that you will recognize that you are dreaming when it occurs. Remind yourself to look at your hand for a sign of awakeness.

10. Recall the plot change or the magical device you thought would be helpful in your dream (see step 7 above). Resolve to take it with you into your dream. Visualize and describe in words the object or the change as you drift off.

Lucid dreamers report that their dreams take on a particular vividness once they become self-aware in a dream. They also often experience a new sense of freedom—not just from nightmares, but from many constraints and fears of daily life. Some phobics have even experienced a decrease in deep-seated waking fears—of heights, say, or dogs—after confronting them in lucid dreams. Of course the technique is not a cure-all for life's problems. Not all your dreams can be lucid, either. About 10% of the population dreams lucidly on a regular basis without working on the technique; these people report about one lucid dream per month. Practice with the faith that you can learn to achieve lucid dreaming and summon the experience when needed.

Lucid dreaming does not have to be use exclusively with nightmares. Another dreamer reported using lucidity to simply explore a pleasant but mysterious image of a blond, tall, tan man who kept cropping up in her dreams, smiling. She discovered that the man was her reflection, and that he appeared at times whe she felt great amounts of competence and self esteem. The blond man reinforced her feeling of power, and she would awaken feeling renewed and strong.

What are the signs that lucidity is happening for you? Phyllis Koch-Sheras, Ann Hollier, and Brooke Jones in their book, *Dream On*, suggest that you look for the following cues:

- When you begin examining your dream environment more critically, such as with recognition of characters or objects from previous dreams
- When you begin thinking about your dream symbols and what they mean *while you are dreaming*
- When you begin to look for signs that what you are experiencing is a dream

A Word of Caution

If you feel that these lucid techniques are not working for you, do not succumb to feelings of failure and give up on dreaming altogether. Remember that it takes time to achieve the mindset and level of awareness you need to experience lucid dreaming at will. What's more, even when you've begun to dream lucidly, you might be misled by the idea of "controlling" your dreams completely. It might not work simply to tell the monster to go away. Maybe you need to ask it harder questions, such as, "Are you my mother?" Maybe you need to ask it for help, or simply demonstrate your resolve and courage by staring it in the eyes. The idea is to cooperate with your dreams rather than to control them. You want to control your own behavior rather than the dream content, as Dr. Joseph Dane at the University of Virginia advises. In this way, you can allow the dream agenda to freely present itself.

Conversing with your dream characters may begin a process of integrating them into your waking life, so that you become less fearful of them and consequently less fearful and anxious while awake. Jayne Gackenbach and Jane Bosveld, in their book *Control Your Dreams*, explain that if you "battle" with dream characters, it may only bury the problem deeper. Ideally, you want to confront your dream fears in a positive way. This serves as a desensitizing process, fortifying you to confront them in your waking life. Dealing directly with your dream conflicts and anxieties in an assertive manner is a sort of "role play" for dealing assertively with difficulties in life. It reminds you that you have the power to reframe the way you see the circumstances you find yourself in—whether awake or asleep. If you choose to practice reframing your dreams situations in your unconscious life, you will be building your ability to reframe situations in your waking life.

Learning to experience awareness and control of your dreams is a skill that improves with practice. If you know that bad dreams are disrupting your sleep, don't be reluctant to experiment with the powerful effects of managing your dreams.

Further Reading

Faraday, Ann, Dr. *Dream Power.* New York: Berkley Books, 1980.

Gackenbach, Jayne; Jane Bosveld. *Control Your Dreams.* New York: Harper and Row, 1989.

Garfield, Patricia, Ph.D. *Creative Dreaming.* New York: Ballantine Books, 1974.

Koch-Sheras, Phyllis; E. Ann Hollier; Brooke Jones. *Dream On: A Dream Interpretation and Exploration Guide for Women.* Englewood Cliffs, N.J.: Prentice-Hall, Inc., 1983.

LaBerge, Stephen. *Lucid Dreaming: The Power of Being Awake and Aware in Your Dreams.* New York: Ballantine Books, 1985.

13

Aging and Sleep

By Dr. Wilse Webb

This chapter is about the natural changes in sleep that occur with aging. Many of us, as we grow older, find ourselves not sleeping as well as we did when we were younger. Knowing what kinds of changes are typical can help you decide whether your own sleep patterns have evolved naturally, or whether your sleep difficulties warrant special attention. In either case, this chapter offers information and suggestions to ease the discomfort that comes with changing sleep habits.

Let me begin by telling you how I have come to view sleep on the basis of more that 30 years of my own research, and my reading of the "thousand eyes of others" who have studied sleep.

I believe that sleep is a natural and effective system that has evolved over life's history in this world. The anvil of nature hammered out an unlearned, self-regulating system of behavior that is necessary and useful in our lives.

Sleep is like walking. We don't have to learn to walk. If the human infant was simply kept alive, without training, it would begin to walk erect and effectively and would experience all the benefits associated with walking. Similarly, human infants left without instruction would end up sleeping like all other human adults. They would have a long sleep period at night of about seven to eight hours and be awake during the day. But just as parental coaching can help us walk earlier in our lives, many people benefit from instruction in proper sleep technique. There are two major "controls" of the sleep system. There is a sleep "need," generally seven to eight hours a day, and a timed "regulator" of this need. In this case of human adults, the need is timed to occur at about the same time each night.

These two major controls are modified by four factors: species, brain regulators, individual differences, and age.

In regard to species, rats sleep like rats, cats sleep like cats, and elephants sleep like elephants. For each species there are different sleep need levels and timings of those needs.

Sleep is also modified by brain conditions. For example, drugs can modify sleep needs. Certain brain anomalies or damage can modify sleep needs and time. The disease narcolepsy, for instance, drastically modifies the timing of sleep.

Within any species even with healthy brain conditions, there is a wide range of individual differences in sleep need. Some humans have a natural need for five hours of sleep a day, and others have a need for 10 hours.

The two major control factors, sleep need and timed regulation, are both affected by aging. Aging spreads out individual differences in these factors. And aging leads to various physiological changes that work to alter a lifetime of ingrained sleep behavior.

Before focusing on older individuals, let's look at sleep changes across the life span. Sleep need, the first control, undergoes dramatic changes over the course of a lifetime. At birth, infants average about 16 hours of sleep per 24 hours, with a range from about 12 to 20 hours. This amount diminishes rapidly. By the end of the first year the average is about 14 hours, and by the fifth year it is about 12 hours. The rate declines more gradually throughout the teens, until adult levels of some seven to eight hours are established. I will detail the changes of further aging shortly.

Even more dramatic are the changes in the second control timing, of sleep. Within the first few weeks (to the great relief of parents), sleep begins to consolidate into a long nighttime period of about 10 hours, with decreasing night awakenings. The diminishing amount of sleep noted above is primarily the result of decreasing daytime sleep or naps. In the first year, children typically need two naps; the "morning" nap is usually abandoned first and, by the fifth year, the afternoon nap is let go.

Young adults might be seen as sleep "athletes" at their maximum sleep capacities. Typically, there is a fully consolidated nighttime sleep period of about seven to eight hours, with a natural "need" ranging from about five to 10 hours. Naps are used primarily to make up for missed nighttime sleep. Again, these patterns are natural and inherent, following a set of built-in rules. As with walking, we can modify the flow of these trends within limits. We cannot make major changes.

And now the primary topic: sleep in older individuals.

It should not come as a surprise that older people do not sleep as they did in their twenties. Along with changing waistlines, receding hairlines, increasing golf handicaps, and flourishing wrinkles, sleep behaviors take on new shape. These changes begin gradually in the thirties and accelerate in pace with increasing age. The following changes are most commonly associated with aging sleep.

1. Beginning in the late fifties there is a general tendency to increase the total amount of sleep needed. Interestingly, a smaller percentage of individuals begin to need *less* sleep at this time. In a group of 90-year-olds, 25 percent to 30 percent were sleeping more than nine hours a day, but 5 percent were sleeping less than five hours. This was in contrast to a group of 30-year-olds, of whom about 2 percent slept more than nine hours, and 3 percent less than five hours. Each extreme—more than nine hours and less than five—became more common with age.

2. Awakening during the night is one of the most common effects of aging on sleep. As measured in the laboratory, some 40 percent of the males and 20 percent of the females between the ages of 50 and 70 were awake more that 30 minutes during the night. Less than 3 percent of the younger persons display this amount of awake time.

3. There is an increase in sleep onset problems, particularly among women. In one laboratory study, about one third of 60-year-old women took longer than 30 minutes to get to sleep; only one fifth of the men had similar difficulties.

4. There is some increase in napping, although this is not universally true among 60-year-olds. About one third of older people do not nap and another third nap only occasionally.

There is a wide range of individual difference in the sleep response to aging. The time of onset of difficulties varies, as does the degree of change experienced. Some older people will increase the sleep amounts, and others decrease; some will have sleep onset problems, and others will not; some will have many and prolonged awakenings, and others will not.

How can you interpret these findings, and what can you do about them? First, it is important to note that the changes described above occur in generally healthy individuals. They are part of the natural process of getting older. The best evidence suggests that these changes result from a diminished capacity of the control of the sleep timing system. When you are young, the control system for sleep timing aids you in getting to sleep and maintaining sleep throughout the night. As you grow older, it becomes less capable of doing so. It's just like not being able to run as fast or as far, or to hit a golf ball as far or as accurately; you can no longer count on your sleep timing system to work as well.

To this natural decrease in your capacity to control sleep, there are added problems. Sleep can be interfered with by other unfortunate accompaniments of aging. There is pain associated with such problems as arthritis, or age-associated increases in sleep apnea, and inabilities to sleep in comfortable positions due to weight. Frequent waking to go to the bathroom is a common problem, another failure of the body's timing system. And, of course, there are other concerns that may accompany aging, such as financial worries.

Older people are certainly aware of their sleep problems. In a broad sample, 30 percent of the women and 20 percent of the men who were 65 years old or older said that they "often" or "always" had difficulty in maintaining sleep through the night. This was approximately double the rate of younger respondents.

But do these figures reflect significant sleep "problems"? This is not a simple question to answer. First, there is a wide discrepancy between physiological measures of sleep and individual evaluations of sleep. Laboratory studies have shown that individuals are poor subjective evaluators of their sleep. Within non-pathological subjects few people can accurately estimate how long or how frequently they awaken during the night. Subjective evaluations are greatly affected by such factors as the degree of change from earlier sleep patterns, beliefs about how others sleep or how they themselves should sleep, and general feelings of well being.

A better question is not whether there are apparent changes in sleep, but whether these changes affect your waking behavior. The effects of not getting enough sleep are clear and straightforward. You will be sleepy during the day when you don't want to be. You will feel sleepy in the morning when you get out of bed. You will nod off when you are reading or looking at television. If these problems are not prominent, then your sleep problems are annoyances rather than real "problems." Only if sleepiness is a prominent daytime problem are the aging sleep changes real "problems."

But whether or not sleep is a "problem" or an "annoyance"—and not being able to get to sleep or waking up after you are asleep can be a real "annoyance"—you still want to be as helpful to your sleep as possible. The following are some tips on sleep hygiene for older people. More general guidelines—on diet, bedroom atmosphere, exercise, and other relevant factors—can be found in Chapter 3.

1. Timing of sleep is the major problem of aging sleep. You need to be as regular as possible in your sleep timing. Try to be in bed, ready for sleep, at about

the same time each night. Even more importantly, try to get up in the mornings at the same time.

2. Don't try to get more sleep than you body needs. If you are having trouble getting to sleep, your body may be telling you that you have extra waking hours in you. Try going to sleep later for a few days—and take advantage of your longer days.

3. If you feel you are not getting enough sleep (you are sleepy during the day), take naps. However, do *not* take naps of longer than one hour, and do not take naps after 4:00 in the afternoon. If you're suffering from chronic insomnia, it's a good idea to avoid naps altogether. (See Chapter 3 for more on napping.)

4. When you wake up at night, don't "fight" to go back to sleep. Don't fill the time with worries, either. Sleep will naturally recur if given a chance (sleep is like love; pursued too strenuously, it will evade you). If "worries" take over, you might get up and do some "duties" before going back to bed. But don't do anything that is likely to keep you up long. (See Chapter 10 for ideas on nighttime activities, and Chapters 6 through 8 for strategies on managing worries. The stimulus control treatment program described in Chapter 9 can be useful to you if tossing and turning wakefully has become part of your bedtime routine.)

5. Don't depend on sleeping pills. Use them only rarely, in desperation, rather than as a general solution. They won't cure the problem: in fact, they'll make it worse. (See Chapter 5 for more on medications.)

6. Rituals are as useful for older people as they can be for children in separating "wake time" from sleep time." A glass of milk, a final TV program, a prayer (even "Now I lay me down to sleep…"), familiar reading: all can help set apart your sleep time and cue your body to drowsiness.

7.   An exercise routine is therapeutic throughout life. A long walk, a game of golf, a gentle-movements dance class, or the swimming you've always enjoyed: any of these can refresh your daytime energy, and make your body ready for nighttime sleep. Although older bodies can't take the pounding younger bodies can, aerobic activity (raising your heartrate for periods of 15 to 20 minutes) is still beneficial for many older people. Stretching before bed can also relieve joint and muscle pains and relax tight muscles. Consult your doctor for suggestions on activities that might be right for you.

A final note. I have been describing the natural changes in sleep that occur in healthy aging persons. Substantial and debilitating changes in sleep can also occur in older persons. Age does not exempt you from prolonged insomnia or disrupted patterns of sleep described in earlier chapters. Indeed the more fragile system of the older person may have increased susceptibility to more severe sleep disorders. When the inability to sleep is prolonged beyond tolerance; when sleep is severely disrupted; when pain and physical problems extensively interfere with sleep and the consequences erupt into daytime life, then one must seek professional help. Chapter 4, *Sleep Disorders,* can help you identify signs of particular sleep disorders. Much of the information in that chapter is particularly relevant to older individuals.

Sleep is a natural and effective system which, given half a chance, functions well. This is generally true even in older persons, when the system shows natural declines in its capacity to control sleep. No, you don't sleep as you did when you were younger. But these variations don't have to have a great effect on daily living, and you can treat them as you treat wrinkles—with wry resignation.

14

Sleep and Chronic Pain

By Dr. Charles M. Morin with Dr. Sandy E. Gramling

Insomnia and Chronic Illness

Sleep is often one of the first casualties of physical ailments. Not surprisingly, insomnia is one of the most widespread complaints among patients with chronic medical illnesses and particularly in those with pain-related conditions. In fact, pain and insomnia are respectively the two most prevalent health complaints brought to the attention of health professionals. While 15 to 30 percent of the general population complains of insomnia, more than half of those suffering from chronic pain conditions describe themselves as "poor sleepers." For many people, therefore, chronic pain means chronic sleep disturbances. Problems falling asleep, frequent wakings in the middle of the night, and premature awakening in the morning are the most common sleep problems. Tossing and turning all night along with bouts of light interrupted sleep further trouble many chronic pain sufferers.

Many chronic illnesses, particularly the pain syndromes, can impair sleep. Disturbed sleep is especially frequent in people suffering from arthritis, osteoporosis, fibrositis, low back pain, temporo-mandibular joint dysfunction, and headaches, to name a few. It is also a common problem associated with chronic illnesses such as cancer and diabetes as well as with renal, cardiovascular, and chronic obstructive pulmonary diseases. Acute illness or injury can cause temporary sleep disturbances as it runs its natural course. Many treatments, either medical or surgical, can also trigger sleep problems as a secondary effect. For example, insomnia is almost always associated with the emotional distress that comes before a stressful medical procedure. Clearly, sleep problems associated with chronic pain and illness are widespread and their impact on one's waking life can be very detrimental.

Consequences of Sleep Disturbances

Disturbed sleep pattern is one of the most disabling consequences of chronic pain. In turn, the consequences of sleep disturbances on daytime functioning can be very distressing as well. Daytime fatigue, lower energy, mood disturbances, and diminished performance represent only a few of these by-products. The daytime problems experienced by pain patients who are poor sleepers are not simply due to their pain. Frequently, poor sleep can worsen impairments in other areas of functioning for pain patients.

Difficulty sleeping in and of itself can have adverse effects on the quality of one's life. Learning to cope with a sleep problem is made even more difficult, however, when it occurs along with medical conditions such as chronic pain or other chronic illnesses. Pain, sleep, and the quality of daytime functioning (emotional well-being, productivity, cognitive abilities) are all interrelated, as this drawing indicates:

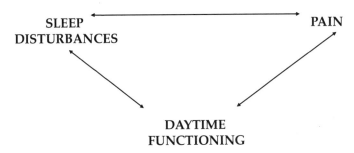

When both pain and sleep problems occur together, the negative effects on daytime functioning may be more severe than the sum of the individual problems. For example, pain patients who also experience poor sleep report more mood problems and impairment in their daytime activities than people suffering from pain without accompanying insomnia.

An important implication of the interrelated nature of pain, sleep, and daytime functioning is that this relationship can go in more than one direction. For example, not only can pain and sleep problems combine to affect daytime functioning adversely, but the cause and effect relationships can move around the circle in the other direction as well. A person who does not get a good night's sleep will often find his or her pain more intense and unpleasant and have more difficulty coping with his or her medical condition during the day. Similarly, negative daytime events such as stressful emotional experiences can interfere with sleep, which in turn may lower pain tolerance.

Fortunately, this vicious cycle can be short-circuited to allow a person with chronic pain or illness to get the nightly sleep he or she needs. This chapter describes self-management techniques that can help you find

more effective methods for coping with sleep disturbances. As a result of better sleep, daytime functioning
and the general quality of life often improve as well.

Origins of Sleep Disturbances

Insomnia and Hospitalization

Sometimes a transient sleep problem that seems to
be caused by a situational stressor does not resolve
itself and develops into a full-fledged case of chronic
insomnia. People suffering from chronic pain and other
chronic illnesses are especially vulnerable to this type
of progression in their sleep problems, particularly if
they are hospitalized. Disruption of the sleep cycle in
hospitalized patients is routine; not surprisingly then,
insomnia is one of the most frequent complaints of
hospital patients. Of course, acute pain is a common
cause of insomnia in this setting, but there are many
other factors affecting hospitalized patients that may
lead to the development of persisting sleep problems
following discharge.

Hospitals are very noisy environments and patients
may be inadvertently awakened at night by roommates, staff, noisy equipment, radio and TV, lights, and
more. In addition, patients are often deliberately
awakened by staff for a variety of scheduled procedures (e.g., blood samples, medications) which must be
performed at fixed intervals. People often compensate
for nighttime awakenings with daytime napping. On a
short-term basis, this is a very useful strategy. In the
long run, however, routine daytime napping can be
detrimental to a good night's sleep because napping
disrupts the natural sleep/wake cycle of the body.
When nighttime awakening due to noise or medical

procedures is no longer a problem, sleeping during the day will make it difficult to sleep at night.

Hospitalization may also be associated with emotional distress, including anxiety, depression, and feelings of helplessness, all of which can inhibit your ability to sleep. A patient who comes to associate the bed with anxiety and discomfort may have difficulty sleeping in bed long after discharge. This "conditioned insomnia" is worsened by the unhealthy sleep habits often acquired in the hospital. When you are confined to a hospital bed, you begin to associate the bed with many daytime activities (e.g., eating, reading, writing letters) that are incompatible with sleeping. Therefore, the bed becomes your cue for arousal and wakefulness rather than the usual cue for relaxation and rest. Continued use of the bed for activities incompatible with sleep makes it increasingly difficult for you to fall asleep in bed when you want to. (See Chapter 9 for more on conditioning insomnia.)

Pain Behaviors Interfering with Sleep

Even without the stressful experience of hospitalization, you can also condition yourself into similarly poor sleep habits without even realizing it. Chronic pain sufferers often develop methods for coping with the discomfort of pain or with its associated physical limitations. While these pain coping strategies allow you to get through your days, they can also have long-term detrimental effects on your sleep pattern.

Bedrest is the most common method used to alleviate pain. Spending excessive amounts of time lying down attempting to relax, rest, nap, or simply find a comfortable body position may interfere with nighttime sleep. Although bedrest is often recommended and does provide needed rest in the short term, too much time spent in bed may yield undesirable effects. It usually leads to fragmented rather than continuous sleep and blocks or prevents healthy rest in the long run.

Using the bed or bedroom as the center of your universe is another natural but detrimental way of coping with physical limitations associated with pain-related conditions. Some people organize their entire daily activities around their bedrooms. Eating, reading, watching TV, paying the bills, and talking on the phone are just a few examples of sleep incompatible activities. The problem is that, when you engage regularly in these activities in your bedroom, the bedroom environment becomes associated with wakefulness rather than with sleepiness.

Sleeping late in the morning or making up an extra hour of sleep whenever you have the chance is also likely to cause problems when it becomes habitual. The incidental sleep may provide a temporary escape from the unpleasant experience of pain. You may even feel refreshed after an extra hour of sleep. But taking naps and maintaining an irregular sleep schedule will disrupt your body's natural rhythm and worsen your nighttime sleep pattern.

The important point to remember is that even though pain, illness, or the psychological stress surrounding hospitalization may have been the main factor initially causing your insomnia, there are several behavioral factors currently maintaining your sleep problem. Although most of these behavior patterns are effective and often the only viable alternative in the short term (e.g., bed rest for acute pain), they exacerbate sleep disturbances in the long run. As much as possible, then, you need to take measures to:

1. Avoid prolonged bed rest
2. Curtail non-sleeping activities in the bedroom
3. Stay on a regular schedule, avoid naps, and get up at a regular time

Now that you have learned about some factors that can disrupt your sleep, it is time to evaluate the nature, time course, and severity of your sleep problem.

Evaluation of Sleep Disorders

Sleep Diary Monitoring

Keeping track of your sleep habits is an important part of gaining a better understanding of your sleep problem. At the end of Chapter 3, you'll find a sample sleep diary. Make several copies of it, and try monitoring your sleep pattern for at least one week. Fill in answers each morning, as part of your daily routine.

Maintaining a daily sleep diary serves several purposes. First, it helps you evaluate the severity of your sleep problem. You may realize after a few days of self-monitoring that you get more sleep than you initially thought. This increased awareness may reduce your anxiety and consequently alleviate your sleep problem. If not, establishing a baseline gives you some perspective on your initial problem as you progress through the treatment plan. As sleep improves, some people tend to lose track of how poor it was before treatment and therefore do not realize how much progress they have made.

Keeping a sleep diary also provides you with a better understanding of how your sleep patterns change over time. There may be great night-to-night variations in your sleep pattern; that is, in fact, more the rule than the exception. The sleep diary can also help pinpoint factors that lead to poor sleep and those that are more conducive to a good night's sleep. Finally, the sleep diary is an excellent tool for monitoring your progress throughout treatment. For all these reasons, it's a good idea to apply yourself conscientiously as you embark upon your sleep management program.

Sleep Laboratory Evaluation

Should you be evaluated in a sleep clinic? An overnight sleep evaluation can be a valuable experience, providing you the most comprehensive assessment of your sleep disorder. The sleep test, called a polysomnogram, can yield valuable information for those suffering from pain and insomnia. It is essential test for diagnosing several sleep disorders such as sleep apnea, narcolepsy, or periodic leg movements during sleep (see Chapter 4 for more information about these disorders).

Before you are scheduled for an overnight sleep evaluation, you will be asked to keep a sleep diary for one to two weeks. You'll then review your diary with a sleep specialist (a psychologist, physician, or both). Your detailed sleep history will be reviewed along with information pertaining to your current sleep-wake schedule, physical problems, medication/substance use, and psychological status. This information helps establish a preliminary diagnosis and initial recommendations, and guides the clinician in deciding whether an overnight evaluation is warranted.

Sleep clinics have several private bedrooms available for overnight evaluations. Special care is taken for these bedrooms to look like hotel rooms (with TV and private bathroom) rather than hospital rooms. It is important to provide an environment as much like home as possible. On the night of the evaluation, you arrive at the clinic two hours before your usual bedtime. A sleep technician prepares you for the sleep test. Small electrodes (sensors) are attached to the head and skin so that sleep, respiration, heart rate, and leg movements can be monitored continuously throughout the night. You go to bed at your usual bedtime in a private bedroom. The technician monitors your sleep from an adjacent control room. This sleep evaluation is non-invasive and there is nothing painful to worry about. While you may wonder how you can sleep under such conditions, people can move around almost as freely as if they were sleeping at home without any equipment. It may take longer to fall asleep because you are in a strange environment, but some insomniacs actually fall asleep more quickly because the cues that keep them awake at home are not present in the sleep laboratory. If you need to go to the bathroom during the sleep study, you can call the technician via an intercom and the test is easily interrupted momentarily. The sleep study lasts only as long as your typical night's sleep at home. The technician wakes you up at your usual arising time. After the study is completed, it takes just a few minutes to remove the electrodes and you are ready to return home or to work.

A one-night polysomnogram will generate about 1000 pages of paper. This data is scored by a sleep technician and used to document how much time was spent in the different stages of sleep as well as any abnormalities in respiration and leg movements. The results are analyzed by a sleep specialist, who then reviews the test results with you and makes appropriate treatment recommendations.

When should you have a sleep test? There are several reasons why you might want to undergo an overnight sleep evaluation. For example, if you wake up with cramps in your calves at night, or your bedpartner has noted leg jerks during your sleep, you may suffer from a condition called *nocturnal myoclonus*. As your leg twitches, you may wake up repetitively at night without remembering it on the following day. This condition can either cause problems maintaining sleep at night or impair your ability to stay awake during the day. It is often accompanied by restless legs at bedtime *(restless leg syndrome)*. Nocturnal myoclonus is a common problem in people suffering from chronic pain and particularly in those whose pain radiates down to the lower extremities. It is also common in those with chronic illnesses such as renal disease and in medical conditions causing poor blood circulation (e.g., diabetes).

If you are sleepy during the day, you are overweight, you snore, and your bedpartner has noticed pauses in your breathing during sleep, this may be an indication that you have *sleep apnea*—a breathing disorder occurring during sleep. Sleepers with apnea may stop breathing 200 to 300 times in a single night, yet be unaware of it. The most direct consequence of sleep apnea is chronic sleep fragmentation, which leads to severe difficulties staying awake during the day. Complications can also arise from continued interruption in air intake. Sleep apnea is particularly frequent in middle-aged men. You'll find more about it and other disorders in Chapter 4.

If after diligently following the treatment program described in this chapter you still have problems sleeping at night, there may be some other sleep disorders of which you are unaware and that could only be detected by an overnight sleep evaluation. You may require additional treatment or a different intervention than that presented in this book.

Pain and Sleep Physiology

Polysomnography has enhanced our understanding of sleep disturbances associated with chronic pain. In fibrositis and similar pain conditions, specific features of the sleep physiology are impaired. Alpha rhythms, a particular brain-wave pattern associated with a mental state of relaxed wakefulness, occur just before sleep onset and are relatively infrequent during sleep in pain-free individuals. In pain sufferers, alpha brain-waves tend to persist into their sleep and particularly into delta or deep sleep. As a result of this intrusion, sleep quality is greatly reduced. Because deep sleep is constantly interspersed with this alpha rhythm throughout the night, the patient gets up in the morning with muscle aches, stiffness, and the feeling of having spent the entire night in a constant light sleep without ever having achieved deep sleep. These physiological features of sleep affect pain perception: a high proportion of alpha waves during sleep is associated with an increase in pain sensation and a decrease in energy level. Conversely, a greater amount of delta waves (deep sleep) without alpha intrusion is associated with a decrease in pain intensity and an increase in energy level. Recent research has shown that pain can be induced in people who are otherwise pain-free by selectively depriving them of deep sleep. These people wake up in the morning reporting muscle ache and stiffness—reproducing symptoms similar to fibrositis. Clinically this phenomena of alpha-delta sleep has been observed in other pain-related conditions as well (arthritis, low back pain, etc).

Coping Strategies for Overcoming Insomnia

Most treatment methods described earlier in this book can help improve your sleep pattern. In this section, self-management skills specifically designed for patients suffering from chronic pain and sleep disturbances are presented. The ultimate goal of this self-management program is to help you regain control over your sleep patterns. It may not completely cure your insomnia, but it can help you cope more effectively with the occasional poor night's sleep almost everyone experiences once in a while. The two main components to this treatment involve (a) changing maladaptive sleep *habits* and (b) rethinking your *beliefs* and attitudes about sleeplessness.

Changing Poor Sleep Habits

By now you are probably aware of several unhealthy habits that may interfere with your sleep. Maintaining irregular sleep schedules, napping, spending excessive amount of time in bed, and using the bed and/or bedroom for non-sleeping activities are the most common *maladaptive* coping strategies used by those suffering from insomnia and pain. The first step of this program consists of breaking these poor behavior patterns disrupting your sleep.

Go to bed only when you're sleepy. There is no reason for going to bed if you are not sleepy. It only gives you more time to worry about your inability to sleep and reinforces the negative associations between the bedroom surroundings and sleeplessness.

Get out of bed if you can't sleep. When you are unable to fall asleep or return to sleep within 10 to 15 minutes, go to another room and engage in some quiet activity. Do not sleep on the couch. Return to bed only when sleepy. Repeat this step as often as necessary throughout the night. Consistent adherence to this regimen will help reassociate your bed and bedroom with getting to sleep quickly. (Chapter 10 offers ideas for appropriate late night activities.)

Maintain a regular arising time. Set the alarm clock and get out of bed at the same time every morning (weekdays and weekends) regardless of the amount of sleep obtained the previous night. Although it may be tempting to stay in bed later because you didn't sleep well the night before, try to maintain a steady sleep/ wake schedule. It helps regulate your internal biological clock and synchronize your sleep/wake rhythm.

Use the bed or bedroom for sleep only. Do not read, eat, watch TV, work, or worry in your bed or bedroom either during the day or at night. Sex is the only exception to this rule. By curtailing non-sleeping activities in the bed and bedroom, you will strengthen the cuing properties of this environment for sleep. Just as you may have developed strong associations between the kitchen and hunger or between a particular chair and relaxation, you want to reinforce the associations between your bedroom and sleep.

Avoid daytime napping. When you stay awake all day, you are more sleepy at night. If a nap is unavoidable, limit it to one hour per day and schedule it before 3:00 p.m. in order to minimize interference with nighttime sleep.

Allow yourself at least one hour before bedtime to unwind. Use this transitional period to engage in your pre-bedtime rituals (e.g., reading, bathing, brushing teeth). Do not rehash events of the day or plan tomorrow's schedule. Schedule another time during the day or early evening to do problem solving and to write down worries and concerns. After a sleepless night, minimize problem-solving on the following day as everything will seem more complicated or more difficult to handle than it really is.

Sleep Restriction. Bedrest is the most common strategy used to cope with both pain and sleep disturbances. While it is an effective and sometimes the only alternative method of dealing with acute pain and sleep problems, excessive amounts of time spent in bed may disrupt sleep patterns. Even though you may get the impression that at least you're getting some rest, too much time lying down awake will worsen rather than improve your sleep pattern. Sleep restriction is a new and somewhat paradoxical method of treating chronic insomnia. This treatment method was designed by Art Spielman, a psychologist at City College of New York, and consists of curtailing the amount of time spent in bed to the actual amount of sleep you get. You need first to determine how much time per night you typically spent in bed and how much of that time is spent asleep. Then you curtail your time in bed to the actual amount of sleep. Here is how it works. After you have kept a sleep diary for one week, calculate your nightly average of (a) total sleep time, (b) time spent in bed, and (c) sleep efficiency:

$$\frac{\text{Total Sleep Time}}{\text{Time in Bed}} \times 100 = \text{Sleep Efficiency}$$

For example, if you were getting an average of six hours of sleep per night out of nine hours spent in bed, your sleep efficiency would be 66.7 percent. Your task is then to restrict the amount of time you spend in bed to the actual amount of sleep. In this example, you would initially restrict your time in bed to six hours per night. This is your "sleep window" for the first week of treatment. As your sleep improves, you gradually extend time in bed by adding 20 to 30 minutes to your sleep window every week. As long as your sleep efficiency is greater than 85 percent, you continue increasing time in bed until you reach an optimal sleep duration. If your sleep efficiency decreases below 80 percent, you should decrease time in bed by 20 to 30 minutes for the following week. When sleep efficiency falls between 80 and 85 percent you simply maintain the same time in bed for an additional week. This sleep restriction procedure will help consolidate your sleep at night. Initially, you may feel more sleepy during the day—don't worry, this is normal. Because you will be sleep deprived, you will also fall asleep faster and sleep deeper at night. Sleep restriction is particularly effective for those whose insomnia is secondary to chronic pain because pain sufferers generally spend large amounts of time in bed resting, napping, or simply trying to find a comfortable body position.

Changing Your Beliefs and Attitudes About Sleep

As you implement these behavioral changes into your new lifestyle, it is critical that you also examine your beliefs and attitudes about sleep and insomnia. Self-imposed pressure to achieve certain sleep standards, excessive concerns about the consequences of poor sleep, and false assumptions about sleep can feed into your sleeping problem. If you can change your unrealistic expectations regarding sleep requirements, challenge dysfunctional beliefs about the consequences of sleeplessness, and correct misattributions about the causes of insomnia, you will move a long way towards a better night's sleep.

Expectations such as "I must sleep eight hours every night" or "I must fall asleep in minutes" are unrealistic. Sleep needs vary widely among individuals and short sleep is not necessarily pathological. There is no universal standard for sleep duration. Sleep as much as you need to feel rested in the morning and remain alert during the day, but not more. Do not place pressure on yourself to achieve certain sleep standards as this will only increase your anxiety and perpetuate your insomnia. Try not to compare your sleep pattern with your bedmate's. There will always be someone who is taller, wealthier, or sleeps better than you. It is best simply to acknowledge that your bedpartner falls asleep faster or sleeps longer than you do.

Attributions of insomnia to external causes are self-defeating. When you say, "My sleep problem is entirely due to pain," then you assume nothing can be done about improving your sleep unless the pain is removed. By now you have learned that behavioral factors can also exacerbate sleep disturbances even though pain is a significant contributing factor. Thus it is important that you adopt a more constructive approach to beating insomnia.

Excessive worrying about the daytime consequences of a poor night's sleep only aggravates your problem. Although chronic sleep deprivation does impair daytime functioning, research has shown that performance problems due to insomnia are minimal. When you worry about those presumed consequences, it only makes you more anxious and decreases your tolerance for pain. You also feed into the vicious cycle of insomnia, emotional distress, low pain tolerance, and more disturbed sleep (recall the drawing in this chapter).

Blaming sleep for mood swings, lowered energy, increased pain, and poor daytime performance is counter productive. There are numerous factors, including natural circadian changes, hormonal changes, and aging, as well as stress in other areas of your life, that may cause those problems. So be careful; don't blame it all on lack of sleep.

Catastrophizing after a sleepless night only makes matters worse. Sleep lost is more likely to be distressing if you perceive it as stressful rather than as a challenge. Don't panic after a sleepless night; stay calm and accept the fact you didn't sleep well the night before. The only certain consequence of sleeplessness is that it will eventually lead to sleepiness. Furthermore, there is no need to make up for all sleep loss. Usually one good night's sleep is enough to put you back in shape. The positive coping strategies in Chapter 8 can help you identify your self-defeating thoughts, and turn them into idea more compatible with managing pain and finding sleep.

Coping with Nocturnal Pain

A person in pain faces unique obstacles to a good night's sleep. The immediate saliency of pain is often hard to ignore and many people who suffer from chronic pain report that their pain is the main reason they have difficulty sleeping at night. There is no question that feeling pain makes it harder to relax and let go. Still, it may be inaccurate to say that the pain is entirely responsible for the insomnia. For example, when a person naps during the day and consequently is not very tired at night, it is not the pain alone that is keeping the person awake, but rather the person's poor sleep habits. Thus it is extremely important to implement all the sleep management techniques just described above. Techniques specific to coping with nocturnal pain will not be very useful if implemented separate from the total self-management program.

Relaxation. A variety of relaxation procedures are described in Chapter 6; these techniques can be particularly useful for pain patients having a hard time falling or staying asleep. These exercises have proved useful in the treatment of a variety of disorders including chronic pain. Overly tense muscles are often to blame in a number of pain conditions including low back pain, temporo-mandibular disorders, and headaches. Relaxation exercises produce lower levels of muscle tension and consequently lead to decreased pain levels. Many chronic pain sufferers are not aware of high levels of tension in their muscles until their muscles start to hurt. Tense muscles are a signal from your body telling you to relax. Unfortunately, most people learn to tune this message out and become quite unaware of what their bodies are trying tell them. If you practice progressive muscle relaxation daily, you'll become more aware of high levels of tension in your muscles and be able to relax these muscles *before* they become painful. Lower levels of pain will lead to less disruption of sleep at night. By becoming proficient at the relaxation exercises, you can then derive a double benefit: you'll have more control over daytime pain, and you'll be better able to relax yourself as a sleep induction technique at night.

You may find relaxation training beneficial for its other effects as well. It has proved to be one of the most generally beneficial techniques in the whole array of psychological techniques. Sometimes relaxation exercises are described as psychology's equivalent to aspirin. Learning relaxation techniques gives you a degree of mastery over your body, and this sense of control alone has beneficial effects on your sense of well-being. A note of caution for pain patients using the progressive muscle relaxation training technique: do not tense muscles to the point of pain. Begin these exercises slowly and progress through them gradually.

Imagery. Despite careful adherence to all of the procedures outlined here, there may be some nights when pain intensity interferes with sleep. Fortunately, imagery is an extremely useful pain control technique that can be used in conjunction with relaxation exercises to help induce sleep. Imagery is useful in this context because it diverts your attention from something unpleasant (pain) to a more pleasant image (pain melting like ice). Numerous studies have demonstrated that when people focus their attention on their pain, they report much higher levels of pain intensity and unpleasantness than when they are distracted with another task. In the daytime it is relatively easy to distract yourself or to "take your mind off" the pain. It can be much more difficult to do so at night when there is nothing to do except try to fall asleep. At night, when the lights are off and it gets fairly quiet, the only stimuli to attend to are those created inside your own body. Unless you direct your attention away with images you create in your mind, the stimuli your body creates may be painful and hard to ignore. To create more positive mental images try following the four steps below:

1. *Relax deeply (see Chapter 6).* Practice your relaxation exercises daily so that you can readily become relaxed when you need to.
2. *Imagine your pain.* Once you are proficient at the relaxation exercises, think of an image that represents the particular type, quality, and intensity of your pain. Some examples are pins and needles sticking in the flesh at the site of pain; a searing sun at the point of pain; or a hammer pounding or a vice turning at the site of pain. What's important here is for you to make the image of your pain personally meaningful.
3. *Imagine your pain relief.* Change the image of pain to something pleasant, or at least tolerable. Visualize a therapeutic image or process which represents the release of pain.

   Examples of how the pain images presented in step 2 might be transformed could be snowflakes lying lightly on the skin, which melt away, instead of pins and needles in the flesh; a cooling moon replacing the sun with a gentle, soothing reflection of light; a hammer fading or dissolving away; the vice slowly opening, or becoming caring, massaging hands.

   Remember, conjure up these images while you are in a relaxed state. You do not have to force the images to appear; when you are relaxed, images will come to you. Select the images that are personally meaningful to you and that best depict your pain and its release.
4. *Imagine the positive benefits.* Visualize yourself feeling better, smiling and laughing, moving around freely, enjoying the people and the things around you. Create an image of yourself which is active, positive, and in good health.

Many advocates of imagery training suggest that this type of imagery facilitates communication between mind and body and enhances the healing process. Although the effects of imagery on the healing process are uncertain, they are clearly not detrimental. In fact, they seem particularly helpful for coping with nocturnal pain.

Benefiting from Social Support

Family, Friends, and Work

Chronic pain sufferers are keenly aware that family and friends often fail to provide the type of social support they need or want. This is partly because the debilitating effects of chronic insomnia and chronic pain can be very difficult for others to understand if they have not experienced these problems personally. Unlike an obvious wound or a symptom that others can observe, chronic pain and insomnia are largely internal, subjective experiences. The person suffering from these symptoms generally must tell others for them to notice there is something wrong. Also, the chronic pain patient has to make requests and turn down requests because of his or her symptoms. How these types of interactions (e.g., reporting symptoms, making or turning down requests) are approached is crucial in learning to cope with chronic pain and insomnia. Other people may want to be supportive but may not know what is needed. Consequently, they may offer too much help, or not enough, simply out of ignorance.

Research has shown that insomniacs tend to internalize their emotions and be more introverted than good sleepers. They often spend excessive amounts of time thinking about their problems, which can lead to feelings of frustration, anger, depression, or anxiety. Insomnia sufferers do not always express these emotions or communicate their needs effectively. Anger is often withheld or expressed inappropriately through a passive or an aggressive style. It is difficult to then go to bed with lingering feelings of anger or frustration and still have a good night's sleep. By dealing assertively with other people, you'll be better able to obtain the type of support you need, improve the quality of your relationship with others, and get yourself a good night's sleep.

There are essentially three different styles of relating to others: *passively, aggressively,* and *assertively.* Being assertive means expressing your thoughts, feelings, and needs while respecting those of others. Being passive and/or aggressive makes it difficult for you to communicate effectively with others and can impede your ability to have your needs met.

Passive Style. People who act in a passive style or unassertive style are reluctant to express their needs to others. Passive people are usually non-responders; when they do ask for something, it is usually in an indirect way. The needs of others are consistently placed above the needs of the self. People often adopt a passive style because they are afraid of being rejected. Often they have internalized a belief that they must be perfect; that in order to win the approval of others they must be agreeable and unimposing. For example, Jane is afraid to ask her husband to change his night owl behaviors because he works so hard, even thought she has to rise at 5:00 a.m. to make a train.

A passive style may lead to several problems. Resentment and anger are an almost inevitable consequence of not making your needs known. These negative emotional states can eat away at your peace of mind and diminish the quality of day-to-day living. Anger at not having your own needs met may manifest itself in more disturbed sleep and increased muscle tension and pain. Moreover, being reluctant to make or turn down requests can land you in situations that aggravate your pain or sleep problem. People don't extend invitations or make requests to make your life difficult; they just express their own needs and desires, and assume you'll do the same. Remember, there is nothing imposing about making a request or expressing a need as long as it respects the other person's right to refuse. Finally, most people find it frustrating to interact with a person behaving unassertively. It puts an unfair burden on others to read the mind of a person who does not express his or her needs. The most satisfying relationships are those in which participants feel an equal balance between having their own needs met and meeting the needs of others.

Aggressive Style. People who adopt an aggressive style, the opposite extreme, demand that their needs be met even at the expense of others. They act as if their thoughts, feeling, and needs are the only ones that matter. People who consistently act in an aggressive manner are often fundamentally insecure people. They seem to have internalized the belief that "I must be right" to compensate for feelings of inadequacy. Challenges to that belief are threatening to their self-esteem. For example, Fred faults Jane for needing so much sleep and blames her for curtailing his fun.

There are also problems with the aggressive style. For instance, people who do not respect the thoughts, feelings, and rights of others will alienate others and put them on the defensive. The frustration that often accompanies chronic pain and insomnia may foster an aggressive style. If this describes you, consider the assertive style as a more productive alternative. The aggressive style may hinder the quality of care received because it often leads to unsatisfactory relationships with health care professionals and fosters a doctor shopping strategy. There is a difference between healthy questioning and outright challenging hostility.

Assertive Style. People with an assertive style believe that they have a legitimate right to express their own thoughts, feelings, and needs, while still respecting those of others. People who adopt an assertive style have learned to express their needs directly through words and actions. They are able to listen attentively and truly "hear" the feeling and opinions of others. They can deal with criticism without becoming hostile or defensive. For example, Fred and Jane agree to problem-solve an equitable solution. An assertive style can yield several benefits. Direct communication of feelings and needs fosters supportive relationships at home and at work. Moreover, assertive communication improves quality of services from health care providers. People who ask questions and directly express their feelings and needs regarding their medical treatment set the stage for effective dialogue regarding patient care.

The following vignette describes Jack, a chronic pain patient with insomnia. The vignette is followed by several responses Jack might make. Note the differences in how Jack might respond to his problem.

Vignette. Jack has suffered from chronic low back pain for almost five years and has had chronic insomnia for almost as long. He has always thought that it was the pain that prevented him from being able to sleep at night, but now realizes that there are several other factors that contribute to his poor sleep. He would like to quit using his bed as the "center of his universe," which would include no longer watching late night TV in bed with his wife.

Response 1. Jack gives the TV to his son Mike without telling his wife about his plans. When she acts hurt about his apparent unwillingness to watch TV with her at night Jack says, "Look, I'm the one who is in pain, but you're the one who is always complaining about something. I read it right here in this book, no more watching TV in bed. If I can't watch TV in bed I don't want you doing it either. Now that's that—case closed—no more discussion." This is an example of an aggressive style.

Response 2. Jack makes a number of changes to diminish the extent to which his bed is the center of his universe. For example, he quits writing letters and stops talking on the telephone in bed. However, Jack is reluctant to say anything to his wife about the TV since she seems to enjoy watching the late night shows with him in bed at night. He is afraid that if he mentions anything to his wife about changing their habits she will be angry and not want to do anything with him in the evening. Jack decides that he has made enough changes and so says nothing to his wife and his old habit continues. This is an example of a passive style.

Response 3. Jack would like to implement all the changes he has read about. He realizes that these changes will have a substantial impact on his wife's sleep habits and so he plans a time when it would be convenient to have an open discussion about proposed changes. He says to her at dinner, "I have been reading a book that makes some suggestions I think might help me sleep better at night. I would like to talk to you about it after dinner if that's OK with you." After dinner the two of them sit down together and Jack says,

"I would like to try these changes to see if they help me sleep better at night. I want to know what you think about them because I know these changes will affect you as well." Jack and his wife decide to watch TV in the living room together before retiring for the evening. This is an example of an assertive style.

Social Support Groups

Though relationships at home and work will be more satisfying if you adopt an assertive style, you may still feel a need to interact with people who are experiencing the same types of problems as yourself. Support groups bring together people who share similar experiences, allowing them to empathize with one another and share coping strategies. A support group can provide a safe environment in which to practice new interpersonal skills, receive feedback and advice regarding coping strategies, and hear fresh perspectives on familiar difficulties. Social support groups are usually not places where people commiserate with a "life's a bitch and then you die" philosophy. A support group provides sympathy for problems from a first-person perspective, but it also encourages people to cope adaptively with their limitations and take a positive, proactive stance toward their problems. Social support has proved a very helpful supplement to this self-management program in the treatment of chronic pain and insomnia.

Conclusion

Chronic pain complicates your insomnia problem, as sleep disturbances complicate your experience with pain and illness. But there is a way to regain control and break this cycle. This self-management program is a highly structured regimen that requires time, patience, and commitment if you expect sleep to improve. Psychological research has shown that successful management of insomnia associated with chronic pain requires consistent adherence to this regimen for eight to 10 weeks. The self-management approach implies that you take responsibility for implementing the recommended changes and that you take an active role in the treatment process. Diligent adherence to the clinical procedures is often the key to a successful outcome. You may find that your sleep pattern gets worse the first few nights of practice and that you wake up in the morning feeling more exhausted than usual. Do not get discouraged. With time and repeated practice, your sleep pattern will improve. If you faithfully implement the techniques described in this chapter, but continue to experience insomnia secondary to chronic pain, it is a good idea to consult your physician regarding referral to a sleep clinic and/or a multi-disciplinary pain clinic. You can benefit from the additional support and reinforcement of other patients, as well as careful guidance from health care professionals in correcting any errors or resistance that interfere with the process of regaining control of your sleep.

15

Final Words

Sometimes it will seem that everything you try is fruitless, that your sleep problem relentlessly drags on with no relief in sight. You will ask yourself, "Why even bother to attempt a new technique? It will turn out to be a failure like the rest and I'll be stuck with this stupid problem for life." If you find yourself falling prey to this line of thinking, stop yourself immediately. It will do you no good whatsoever to dwell on the hopelessness of it all. This kind of self-defeating talk only promotes the stance of victimization. If you regard yourself as a victim of poor sleep, leaving yourself no avenues for change, you will remain a victim forever.

This is not to say that your sleep problem will disappear overnight if you simply adjust your attitude. Most likely it will not. But, as with any self-help maneuver, careful persistence on your part will pay off in the long run. Remember these four points when you feel despair over your sleep problem. Read them over and over to bolster your spirit and resolve.

1. **Keep your expectations realistic.** Allow yourself a gradual improvement in sleep. Permit yourself to

develop slowly, over time, healthy sleep strategies. Reward yourself for even seemingly small gains.

2. Treat your problems holistically. Don't expect one sleep technique to "do it all." You are a complex being. Stay open to all the various aspects of your mind, body, and spirit. This means carefully examining your physical needs as well as your emotional well-being.

3. Adopt an attitude of passive concentration. Don't try so hard to fall asleep. Don't tackle every new technique with such zealous fervor that you lose sight of your intention: to turn your mind off and drift off to sleep. Learn to let go.

4. At the same time, don't give up. Be persistent. Learn to concentrate passively on your sleep strategies. This means not forcing the issue, but allowing yourself to be open to better sleep strategies. Commit yourself to healthy sleep.

If all else fails, pretend that this book is a sedative. Tell yourself that every time you read it, pick it up, even glance at it, your eyelids will begin to droop and you will yawn. My faithful husband, offering to read late night drafts of this book before they were shipped off to the publisher the next day, would begin eagerly, and what seemed like minutes later push the chapters aside, yawning, ready for bed. He is an example of a person particularly susceptible to suggestion. You, too, can develop the ability, perhaps not as dramatic, to react positively to certain cues. Keep this book by your bedside, and every time you wake up, look at it and remind yourself that you are in control, you are re-laxed, and you can sleep.

Appendix

Sleep Disorder Centers

Listings are alphabetical by state and in numerical order by ZIP code within each state. If you would like more information, you may write to the American Sleep Disorders Association, 604 Second Street Southwest, Rochester, MN 55902.

Alabama

Sleep Disorders Center of
    Alabama
800 Montclair Road
Birmingham, AL 35213

University of Alabama
Sleep-Wake Disorders Center
University Station
Birmingham, AL 35294

The Children's Hospital of
    Alabama
Sleep Disorders Laboratory
1600 7th Avenue South
Birmingham, AL 35233

Huntsville Hospital
North Alabama Sleep
    Disorders Center
101 Sivley Road
Huntsville, AL 35801

Mobile Infirmary Medical
    Center
Sleep Disorders Center
P.O. Box 2144
Mobile, AL 36652

Alaska

University of Alaska
Attn: Carla Hellerson, M.D.
1919 Lathrop, Drawer 30
Fairbanks, AK 99701

Arizona

Good Samaritan Medical
    Center
Sleep Disorders Center
1111 E. McDowell Road
Phoenix, AZ 85006

Humana Hospital
Sleep Disorders Center
3929 East Bell Road
Phoenix, AZ 85032

University of Arizona
Sleep Disorders Center
1501 North Campbell Avenue
Tucson, AZ 85724

Arkansas

Arkansas Children's Hospital
Sleep Disorders Center
800 Marshall Street
Little Rock, AR 72202

Baptist Medical Center
Sleep Disorders Center
9601 I-630 Exit 7
Little Rock, AR 72205

Sleep Disorders Diagnostic &
   Research Center
4301 W. Markham, Slot 594
Little Rock, AR 72205

California

The Hospital of the Good
   Samaritan
The Sleep Disorders Center
616 South Witmer Street
Los Angeles, CA 90017

UCLA Sleep Disorders Clinic
Department of Neurology
Room 1184 RNRC
710 Westwood Plaza
Los Angeles, CA 90024

Hollywood Presbyterian
   Medical Center
Sleep Disorders Center
1300 North Vermont Street
Los Angeles, CA 90027

Michael H. Bonnet, Ph.D.
2219 Bentley Avenue, #301
Los Angeles, CA 90054

Downey Community Hospital
Sleep Disorders Center
11500 Brookshire Avenue
Downey, CA 90241

Torrance Memorial Hospital
Sleep Disorders Center
3330 Lomita Blvd.
Torrance, CA 90509

Palma Intercommunity
   Hospital
Sleep Disorders Center
7901 Walker Street
La Palma, CA 90623

Huntington Memorial
   Hospital
Sleep Disorders Center
100 Congress Street
Pasadena, CA 91105

Dennis McGinty, Ph.D.
Veterans Administration
   Hospital
16111 Plummer Street
Sepulveda, CA 91343

Holy Cross Hospital
Sleep Disorders Center
15031 Rinaldi Street
Mission Hills, CA 91345

North Valley Sleep Disorders
   Center
11550 Indian Hills Rd., #291
Mission Hills, CA 91345

Southern California Sleep
   Apnea Center
Lombard Medical Group
2230 Lynn Road
Thousand Oaks, CA 91360

Queen of the Valley Hospital
Pediatric Sleep Apnea
   Laboratory
1115 South Sunset Avenue
West Covina, CA 91790

Pomona Valley Hospital
    Medical Center
Sleep Disorders Center
1798 North Garey Avenue
Pomona, CA 91767

Scripps Clinic and Research
    Foundation
Sleep Disorders Center
10666 North Torrey Pines Road
La Jolla, CA 92037

Grossmont District Hospital
Sleep Disorders Center
5555 Crossmont Center Drive
La Mesa, CA 92044

San Diego Regional Sleep
    Disorders Center
Harbor View Medical Center
    and Hospital
120 Elm Street
San Diego, CA 92101

Naval Hospital
Cheryl L. Spinweber, Ph.D.
Behavioral
    Psychopharmacology
Building 36-4
San Diego, CA 92134

116A Veterans Administration
    Medical Center
Sleep Disorders Clinic
3350 La Jolla Village Drive
San Diego, CA 92161

Loma Linda University
    Medical Center
Sleep Disorders Center
11234 Anderson Street
Loma Linda, CA 92354

St. Jude Hospital and
    Rehabilitation Center
Sleep Disorders Institute
101 East Valencia Mesa Drive
Fullerton, CA 92634

Joel B. Younger, M.D.
10532 Wulff Drive
Villa Park, CA 92667

University of California Irvine
    Medical Center
Sleep Disorders Center
101 City Drive South
Orange, CA 92668

South Coast Medical Center
Sleep Disorders Center
31872 Coast Highway
South Laguna, CA 92677

WMCA Sleep Disorders Center
1101 South Anaheim Blvd.
Anaheim, CA 92805

Kaweah Delta District Hospital
Sleep Disorders Center
400 West Mineral King Avenue
Visalia, CA 93291

Antelope Valley Hospital
    Medical Center
Respiratory Sleep Laboratory
1600 West Avenue J
Lancaster, CA 93534

Sequoia Hospital
Sleep Disorders Center
Whipple and Alameda
Redwood City, CA 94062

St. Mary's Hospital
Sleep Disorders Clinic
450 Stanyan Street
San Francisco, CA 94117

Pacific Presbyterian Medical
    Center
Sleep Disorders Center
P.O. Box 7999
San Francisco, CA 94120

Laughton Miles, M.D.
801 Welch Road, Suite 209
Palo Alto, CA 94304

Stanford University Medical
    Center
Sleep Disorders Clinic
211 Quarry Road, N2A
Stanford, CA 94305

William C. Dement, M.D.
440 Gerona Road
Stanford, CA 94305

Merritt-Peralta Medical Center
Sleep Apnea Center
450 30th Street
Oakland, CA 94609

San Jose Hospital
Sleep Disorders Center
675 East Santa Clara Street
San Jose, CA 95112

Sutter Sleep Disorders Lab.
Sutter Hospitals
52nd and F Streets
Sacramento, CA 95819

Richard M. Coleman, Ph.D.
473 Live Oak Drive
Mill Valley, CA 94941
Roger J. Baloch, M.D.
3158 Altamonte Drive
Beale AFB, CA 95903

Colorado

John Zimmerman, Ph.D.
700 Delaware Street
Davis Pavilion
Denver, CO 80204

University of Colorado Health
    Sciences Center
Sleep Disorders Center
700 Delaware Street
Denver, CO 80204

National Jewish Center of
    Immunology and
    Respiratory Medicine
Cardio-Respitory Sleep
    Disorders Center
1400 Jackson
Denver, CO 80206

Porter Memorial Hospital
Sleep Disorders Center
2525 South Downing
Denver, CO 80210

Eric Hoddes, Ph.D.
1801 Williams Street
Suite 300
Denver, CO 80218

Presbyterian Medical Center
Sleep Disorders Center
1719 E. 19th Avenue
Denver, CO 80218

Martin Reite, M.D.
4200 W. 9th Avenue
P.O. Box C268
Denver, CO 80262

Connecticut

The Griffin Hospital
Sleep Disorders Center
130 Division Street
Derby, CT 06418

New Haven Sleep Disorders
   Center
100 York Street
University Towers
New Haven, CT 06511

District of Columbia

Georgetown University
   Hospital
Sleep Disorders Center
3800 Reservoir Road, N.W.
Washington, DC 20007

Florida

Center for Sleep Disordered
   Breathing
P.O. Box 2982
Jacksonville, FL 32203

Baptist Medical Center
Sleep-Related Breathing
   Disorders Center
800 Prudential Drive
Jacksonville, FL 32207

Sacred Heart Hospital
Sleep Disorders Center
5151 North 9th Avenue
Pensacola, FL 32504

Sleep Evaluation Center
University of Miami Medical
   School
Miami, FL 33136

Mt. Sinai Medical Center
Sleep Disorders Center
4300 Alton Road
Miami Beach, FL 33140

Broward General Medical
   Center
Sleep Disorder Laboratory
1600 South Andrews Avenue
Fort Lauderdale, FL 33316

Georgia

Northside Hospital
Sleep Disorders Center
1000 Johnson Ferry Road
Atlanta, GA 30342

Saint Joseph's Hospital
Savannah Sleep Disorders
   Center
11705 Mercy Boulevard
Savannah, GA 31420

Hawaii

Straub Clinic & Hospital
Sleep Disorders Center of the
   Pacific
888 South Kling Street
Honolulu, HI 96813

Idaho

St. Luke's Regional Medical
   Center
Idaho Sleep Disorders Center
190 East Bannock
Boise, ID 83712

Illinois

Howard M. Kravitz, D.O.
8722 N. Springfield Avenue
Skokie, IL 60076

Veterans Hospital
Sleep Disorders Center
Neurology Service
Hines, IL 60141

Evanston Hospital
Sleep Disorders Center
2650 Ridge Avenue
Evanston, IL 60201

Henrotin Hospital
Sleep Disorders Center
111 West Oak Street
Chicago, IL 60610

Robert A. Gross, M.D.
251 E. Chicago Avenue #930
Chicago, IL 60611

Rush-Presbyterian-St. Lukes
Sleep Disorders Center
1753 West Congress Parkway
Chicago, IL 60612

University of Chicago
Sleep Disorders Center
5841 South Maryland, Box 425
Chicago, IL 60637

Methodist Medical Center of
    Illinois
C. Duane Morgan Sleep
    Disorders Center
221 Northeast Glen Oak
Peoria, IL 61626

Carle Regional Sleep
    Disorders Center
602 West University
Urbana, IL 61801

Decatur Memorial Hospital
Center for Sleep-Related
    Breathing Disorders
2300 North Edward
Decatur, IL 62526

Indiana

Winona Memorial Hospital
Sleep Disorders Center
3232 North Meridian Street
Indianapolis, IN 46208

Community Hospitals of
    Indianapolis
Sleep/Wake Disorders Center
1500 North Ritter Avenue
Indianapolis, IN 46219

Lutheran Hospital of Fort
    Wayne
Regional Sleep Studies
    Laboratory
3024 Fairfield Avenue
Fort Wayne, IN 46807

Lafayettte Home Hospital
Sleep Alertness Center
2400 South Street
Lafayette, IN 47903

Iowa

Iowa Methodist Medical
    Center
Sleep Disorders Center
1200 Pleasant Street
Des Moines, IA 50309

University of Iowa Hospital
and Clinics
Sleep Disorders Center
Department of Neurology
Iowa City, IA 52242

St. Luke's Sleep Disorders
Center for Sleep Related
Disorders
1227 E. Rusholme Street
Davenport, IA 52803

Mercy Hospital
Sleep Disorders Center
West Central Park at Marquette
Davenport, IA 52804

Kansas

Wesley Medical Center
Sleep Disorders Center
550 North Hillside
Wichita, KS 67214

Kentucky

Humana Hospital-Audubon
Sleep Disorders Center
One Audubon Plaza Drive
Louisville, KY 40217

St. Joseph's Hospital
Sleep Disorders Center
One St. Joseph Drive
Lexington, KY 40504

Robert Granacher, M.D.
St. Joseph Office Park
1401 Horrodsburg Road
Lexington, KY 40504

Good Samaritan Hospital
Sleep Disorders Center
310 South Limestone
Lexington, KY 40508

University of Kentucky
College of Medicine
Sleep Apnea Laboratory
MN 578, Dept. of Medicine
800 Rose Street
Lexington, KY 40536

Louisiana

Tulane Sleep Disorders Center
1415 Tulane Avenue
New Orleans, LA 70112

Touro Infirmary
Sleep Disorders Center
1401 Foucher
New Orleans, LA 70115

Tulane Medical School
Sleep Disorders Center
Department of Psychiatry and
Neurology
New Orleans, LA 70118

Willis-Knighton Medical
Center
Sleep Disorders Center
2600 Greenwood Road
Shreveport, LA 71103

Louisiana State University
Medical Center
LSU Sleep Disorders Center
P.O. Box 33932
Shreveport, LA 71130

Maine

Sleep Laboratory
Maine Medical Center
22 Bramhall Street
Portland, ME 04102

Maryland

National Capitol Sleep Center
4520 East West Highway, #406
Bethesda, MD 20814

The Maryland Sleep
    Diagnostic Center
Ruxton Towers, Suite 211,
    8415 Bellona Lane,
Baltimore, MD 21204

Johns Hopkins Sleep
    Disorders Center
Hopkins Bayview
    Research Campus
Francis Scott Key
    Medical Center
301 Bayview Boulevard
Baltimore, MD 21224

Sleep Disorders Center
Baltimore City Hospital
Baltimore, MD 21224

Massachusetts

University of Massachusetts
    Medical Center
Sleep Disorders Center
Department of Neurology
Worcester, MA 01605

University of Massachusetts
Sleep-Wake Disorders Unit
55 Lake Avenue, North
    Worcester
Worcester, MA 01605

Sandra Horowitz, M.D.
14 Dartmouth Drive
Framingham, MA 01701

Boston Children's Hospital
Pediatric Sleep Disorders
    Center
300 Longwood Avenue
Boston, MA 02115

Brigham & Women's Hospital
Neuroendocrinology
    Laboratory
221 Longwood Avenue, Room
    505
Boston, MA 02115

Ernest Hartmann, M.D.
170 Morton Street
Boston, MA 02130

Boston University Medical
    Center
Sleep Disorders Center
75 East Newton Street
Boston, MA 02146

Michael P. Biber, M.D.
1269 Beacon Street
Brookline, MA 02146

Beth Israel Hospital
Sleep Disorders Unit
330 Brookline Avenue, KS430
Boston, MA 02215

Michigan

Bloomfield Institute of Sleep
    Disorders
853 Woodward
Pontiac, MI 48053

Sleep Disorders Institute
44199 Dequindre, Suite 403
Troy, MI 48098

VA Medical Center
Sleep/Wake Disorders
    Unit (127b)
Southfield & Outer Drive
Allen Park, MI 48101

Univeristy of Michigan
    Hospitals
Sleep Disorders Center
1500 E. Medical Center Drive
Med Inn C433, Box 0842
Ann Arbor, MI 48109

Henry Ford Hospital
Sleep Disorders Center
2799 W. Grand Boulevard
Detroit, MI 48202

Michigan State University
Department of Medicine
Robert C. Smith, M.D.
8301 Clinical Center
East Lansing, MI 48824

Ingham Medical Center
Sleep Disorders Program
2025 S. Washington Avenue,
    Suite 300
Lansing, MI 48910

Kenneth E. Starz, M.D.
Upjohn Company
7000 Portage Road
Kalamazoo, MI 49001

Minnesota

Abbott Northwestern Hospital
Sleep Disorders Center
800 East 28th Street at Chicago
    Avenue
Minneapolis, MN 55407

Hennepin County Medical
    Center
Minnesota Regional Sleep
    Disorders Center
701 Park Avenue
Minneapolis, MN 55415

Mark Wedel, M.D.
St. Louis Park Medical Center
5000 W. 39th Street
Minneapolis, MN 55416

Methodist Hospital
Sleep Disorders Center
6500 Excelsior Boulevard
St. Louis Park, MN 55426

Fairview Southdale Hospital
Sleep Disorders Center
6401 France Avenue South
Edina, MN 55435

St. Mary's Medical Center
Duluth Regional Sleep
    Disorders Center
407 East Third Street
Duluth, MN 55805

Mayo Clinic
Sleep Disorders Center
200 First Street, S.W.
Rochester, MN 55905

Mississippi

University of Mississippi
    Medical Center
Sleep Disorders Center
2500 North State Street
Jackson, MS 39216

Memorial Hospital at Gulfport
Sleep Disorders Center
P.O. Box 1810
Gulfport, MS 39501

Missouri

St. Louis University Medical
    Center
Sleep Disorders Center
1221 South Grand Boulevard
St. Louis, MO 63104

Deaconess Hospital
Sleep Disorders and Research
    Center
6150 Oakland Avenue
St. Louis, MO 63139

St. Mary's Hospital
Sleep Disorders Center
101 Memorial Drive
Kansas City, MO 64108

Research Medical Center
Sleep Disorders Center
2316 East Meyer Blvd.
Kansas City, MO 64132

L.E. Cox Medical Center
Sleep Disorders Center
3801 S. National Avenue
Springfield, MO 65807

Nebraska

Lutheran Medical Center
Sleep Disorders Center
515 South 26th Street
Omaha, NE 68103

New Hampshire

Dartmouth-Hitchcock Sleep
    Disorders Center
Department of Psychiatry
Dartmouth Medical School
Hanover, NH 03756

Sleep-Wake Disorders Center
Hampstead Hospital
East Road
Hampstead, NH 03841

New Jersey

Newark Beth Israel Medical
    Center
Sleep Disorders Center
201 Lyons Avenue
Newark, NJ 07112

New Mexico

Lovelace Medical Center
Sleep Disorders Center
5400 Gibson Boulevard S.E.
Albuquerque, NM 87108

University of New Mexico
Hospital
Department of Medicine
Wolfgang W.
Schmidt-Nowara, M.D.
Pulmonary Divison 7-South
Albuquerque, NM 87131

New York

Sleep Disorders Center
City College of New York
New York, NY 10031

Columbia-Presbyterian
Medical Center
Sleep Disorders Center
161 Fort Washington Avenue
New York, NY 10032

Mount Sinai Medical Center
Institute for Sleep and Aging
One Gustave Levy Place
New York, NY 10129

Montefiore Hospital
Sleep-Wake Disorders Center
111 East 210th Street
Bronx, NY 10467

New York Hospital—
Cornell Medical Center
Sleep-Wake Disorders Center
21 Bloomingdale Road
White Plains, NY 10605

Winthrop-University Hospital
Sleep Disorders Center
259 First Street
Mineola, NY 11501

State University of New York
at Stony Brook
Sleep Disorders Center
Stony Brook, NY 11794

Sleep Disorders Center
University Hospital
MR 120 A
Stony Brook, NY 11794

St. Josephs Hospital
The Sleep Laboratory
301 Prospect Avenue
Syracuse, NY 13203

Community General Hospital
The Sleep Center
Broad Road
Syracuse, NY 13215

Millard Fillmore Hospital
Sleep Disorders Center of
Western New York
3 Gates Circle
Buffalo, NY 14209

St. Mary's Hospital
Sleep Disorders Center
89 Genesee Street
Rochester, NY 14611

Sleep Disorders Center of
Rochester
2110 Clinton Avenue South
Rochester, NY 14618

North Carolina

Duke University Medical
Center
Sleep Disorders Center
Division of Neurology
Durham, NC 27710

University Memorial Hospital
Sleep Disorders Center
P.O. Box 560727
Charlotte, NC 28256

North Dakota

St. Luke's Hospital
TNI Sleep Disorders Center
Fifth Street at Mills Avenue
Fargo, ND 58102

St. Joseph's Hospital
Sleep Disorders Center
720 Fourth Street North
Fargo, ND 58122

Ohio

Robert W. Clark, M.D.
1450 Hawthorne Avenue
Columbus, OH 43203

The Ohio State University
    Sleep Disorders Treatment
    and Research Center
473 West 12th Avenue
Columbus, OH 43210

The Toledo Hospital
Northwest Ohio Sleep
    Disorders Center
2142 N. Cove Boulevard
Toledo, OH 43606

St. Vincent Medical Center
Sleep Disorders Center
2213 Cherry Street
Toledo, OH 43608

Mt. Sinai Medical Center
Sleep Disorders Center
1800 E. 105th Street
Cleveland, OH 44106

The Cleveland Clinic
    Foundation
    Sleep Disorders Center
9500 Euclid Avenue S53
Cleveland, OH 44195

Bethesda Oak Hospital
Sleep Disorders Center
619 Oak Street
Cincinnati, OH 45206

Cincinnati Sleep Disorders
    Center
515 Melish Avenue
Cincinnati, OH 45229

Jewish Hospital
Sleep Disorders Center
515 Melish Avenue
Cincinnati, OH 45229

The Center for Sleep and
    Wake Disorders
Miami Valley Hospital,
    Suite G200
30 Apple Street,
Dayton, OH 45409

The Center for Research in
    Sleep Disorders
1275 East Kemper
Cincinnati, OH 45426

Sleep Disorders Center
Kettering Medical Center
3535 South Blvd.
Kettering, OH 45429

Oklahoma

Presbyterian Hospital
Sleep Disorders Center
N.E. 13th at Lincoln Boulevard
Oklahoma City, OK 73104

Saint Francis Hospital
Sleep Disorders Center
6161 South Yale
Tulsa, OK 74136

Oregon

Good Samaritan Hospital
Pacific Northwest Sleep
    Disorders Program
1130 N.W. 22nd, Ave., Suite 240
Portland, OR 97210

Rogue Valley Medical Center
Sleep Disorders Center
2825 Barnett Road
Medford, OR 97504

Pennsylvania

West Psychiatric Institute and
    Clinic
Sleep Evaluation Center
3811 O'Hara Street
Pittsburgh, PA 15213

Mercy Hospital of Johnstown
Sleep Disorders Center
1127 Franklin Street
Johnstown, PA 15905

Crozer-Chester Medical Center
Sleep Disorders Center
Department of Neurology
Upland-Chester, PA 19013

Jefferson Medical College
Sleep Disorders Center
1015 Walnut Street, 3rd Floor
Philadelphia, PA 19107

Medical College of
    Pennsylvania
Department of Neurology
Sleep Disorders Center
3200 Henry Avenue
Philadelphia, PA 19129

Rhode Island

Rhode Island Hospital
Sleep Apnea Laboratory
593 Eddy Street, APC 479-A
Providence, RI 02903

A.R. Hamel, Ph.D.
203 Governor Street
Providence, RI 02906

Bradley Hospital
Sleep Lab, Department of
    Psychiatry
1011 Veterans Memorial
    Parkway
East Providence, RI 02915

South Carolina

Baptist Medical Center
Sleep Disorders Center of
    South Carolina
Taylor at Marion Strreets
Columbia, SC 29220

Spartanburg Regional Medical
    Center
Sleep Disorders Center
101 East Wood Street
Spartanburg, SC 29303

Sleep Disorders Center of
    Greenville Hospital System
701 Grove Road
Greenville, SC 29605

Self Memorial Hospital
Children's Sleep Disorders
    Center
1325 Spring Street
Terry Marshall, MD
Greenwood, SC 29646

South Dakota

Sioux Valley Hospital
Sleep Disorders Center
1100 South Euclid
Sioux Falls, SD 57117

Rapid City Regional Hospital
The Sleep Center
353 Fairmont Blvd.
P. O. Box 6000
Rapid City, SD 57709

Tennessee

Saint Thomas Hospital
Sleep Disorders Center
P.O. Box 380
Nashville, TN 37202

West Side Hospital
Sleep Disorders Center
2221 Murphy Avenue
Nashville, TN 37203

Ft. Sanders Regional Medical
    Center
Sleep Disorders Center
1901 West Clinch Avenue
Knoxville, TN 37916

St. Mary's Medical Center
Sleep Disorders Center
Oak Hill Avenue
Knoxville, TN 37917

Baptist Memorial Hospital
Sleep Disorders Center
899 Madison Avenue
Memphis, TN 38146

Texas

Pasadena Bayshore Medical
    Center
Sleep Disorders Center
4000 Spencer Highway
Pasadena, TX 71504

Presbyterian Hospital
Sleep-Wake Disorders Center
8200 Walnut Hill Lane
Dallas, TX 75231

RHD Memorial Medical
    Center
Sleep/Wake Disorders Center
LBJ Freeway at Webbs Chapel
P.O. Box 819094
Dallas, TX 75381

All Saints Episcopal Hospital
Sleep Disorder Diagnostic and
    Treatment Center
1400 8th Avenue
Fort Worth, TX 76104

Scott and White Clinic
Sleep Disorders Center
2401 South 31st Street
Temple, TX 76508

Baylor College of Medicine
Department of Psychology
Sleep Disorders Center
Houston, TX 77030

Sam Houston Memorial
   Hospital
Sleep Disorders Center
8300 Waterbury, Suite 350
Houston, TX 77055

Humana Hospital
   Metropolitan
Sleep Disorders Center
303 McCullough
San Antonio, TX 78212

Sun Towers Hospital
Sleep Disorders Center
1801 North Oregon
El Paso, TX 79902

Utah

LDS Hospital
Intermountain Sleep Disorders
   Center
325 8th Avenue
Salt Lake City, UT 84143

Utah Neurological Clinic
Sleep Disorders Center
1055 North 300 West, Suite 400
Provo, UT 84604

Virginia

Medical College of Virginia
Sleep Disorders Center
P.O. Box 268—MCV Station
Richmond, VA 23298

Eastern Virginia Medical
   School
Sleep Disorders Center
600 Gresham Drive
Norfolk, VA 23507

Community Hospital of
   Roanoke Valley
Sleep Disorders Center
P.O. Box 12946
Roanoke, VA 24029

Washington

Providence Medical Center
Sleep Disorders Center
550 16th Avenue, Suite 304
Seattle, WA 98124

Sacred Heart Medical Center
Sleep Apnea Center
West 101 8th Avenue, TAF-C9
Spokane, WA 99220

Wisconsin

Columbia Hospital
Milwaukee Regional Sleep
   Disorders Center
2025 East Newport Avenue
Milwaukee, WI 53211

St. Mary's Hospital
Sleep/Wake Disorders Center
2320 North Lake Drive
Milwaukee, WI 53211

Gundersen Clinic, Ltd.
Wisconsin Sleep Disorders
   Center
1836 South Avenue
La Crosse, WI 54601

Contributing Authors

Wilse B. Webb, Ph.D. is a Graduate Research Professor at the University of Florida, where he conducts research into the nature of sleep and the aging process. He received his undergraduate degree at Louisiana State University and his masters and doctorate in Psychology at the State University of Iowa. He has been a Cambridge fellow, president of the Southeastern Psychological Association, and president of the American Psychological Association Division of History. Dr. Webb's publications include numerous journal articles spanning a 40 year career, plus seven books on various aspects of sleep, including *Sleep and Dreams* and *Sleep, Aging and Related Disorders.*

James K. Walsh, Ph.D. received his Ph.D. in Physiological Psychology from St. Louis University in 1978. He has been involved in sleep research and sleep disorders medicine since 1976. He currently is Director of the Sleep Disorders and Research Center at the Deaconess Hospital in St. Louis. Dr. Walsh holds the position of Associate Clinical Professor in the Departments of Psychiatry and Pediatrics, as well as Assistant Clinical Professor in the Department of Neurology at the St. Louis University School of Medicine. He is also Adjunct Associate Professor in the Department of Psychology at St. Louis University. He has been certified as an Accredited Clinical Polysomnographer by the American Sleep Disorders Association. Dr. Walsh has published over 60 journal articles and book chapters and has lectured extensively. He has served on the Board of Directors of the American Sleep Disorders Association since 1984 and held the office of Secretary/Treasurer from 1988 until 1990. He is currently President-Elect of the American Sleep Disorders Association.

Charles M. Morin, Ph.D. is a clinical psychologist and Assistant Professor of Psychiatry at Virginia Commonwealth

University. He is Director of the Sleep Disorders Center at the Medical College of Virginia. He obtained his undergraduate education in Quebec, Canada and received his Ph.D. in Clinical Psychology from Nova University, Florida. He completed a residency training at the University of Mississippi Medical Center and was a post-doctoral fellow in Sleep Disorders Medicine at the Medical College of Virginia. Dr. Morin is actively involved in clinical research activities in the sleep disorders field. He has been funded by the National Institute of Mental Health for his research on insomnia. He has published several articles and book chapters and is currently writing a book on the psychological management of insomnia.

Other New Harbinger Self-Help Titles

The Relaxation & Stress Reduction Workbook, 3rd Edition, $13.95

Leader's Guide to the Relaxation & Stress Reduction Workbook, $14.95

Beyond Grief: A Guide for Recovering from the Death of a Loved One, $10.95

Thoughts & Feelings: The Art of Cognitive Stress Intervention, $12.95

Messages: The Communication Skills Book, $11.95

The Divorce Book, $10.95

Hypnosis for Change: A Manual of Proven Techniques, 2nd Edition, $11.95

The Deadly Diet: Recovering from Anorexia & Bulimia, $11.95

Self-Esteem, $11.95

The Better Way to Drink, $10.95

Chronic Pain Control Workbook, $12.50

Rekindling Desire, $10.95

Life Without Fear: Anxiety and Its Cure, $9.95

Visualization for Change, $11.95

Guideposts to Meaning, $10.95

Controlling Stagefright, $10.95

Videotape: Clinical Hypnosis for Stress & Anxiety Reduction, $24.95

Starting Out Right: Essential Parenting Skills for Your Child's First Seven Years, $12.95

Big Kids: A Parent's Guide to Weight Control for Children, $10.95

Personal Peace: Transcending Your Interpersonal Limits, $10.95

My Parent's Keeper: Adult Children of the Emotionally Disturbed, $11.95

When Anger Hurts, $11.95

Free of the Shadows: Recovering from Sexual Violence, $11.95

Resolving Conflict With Others and Within Yourself, $11.95

Liftime Weight Control, $10.95

When Once Is Not Enough, $11.95

Getting to Sleep, $10.95

Send a check or purchase order for the titles you want, plus $2.00 for shipping and handling, to:

New Harbinger Publications
Department B
5674 Shattuck Avenue
Oakland, CA 94609

Or write for a free catalog of all our quality self-help publications.